ECERS-E: The Early Childhood Environment Rating Scale Curricular Extension to ECERS-R

Kathy Sylva   Iram Siraj-Blatchford   Brenda Taggart

Trentham Books
Stoke on Trent, UK and Sterling, USA

Trentham Books Limited

Westview House   22883 Quicksilver Drive
734 London Road   Sterling
Oakhill   VA 20166-2012
Stoke on Trent   USA
Staffordshire
England ST4 5NP

First published 2003
Second edition 2006
Third edition 2010

British Library Cataloguing-in-Publication Data
A catalogue record for this book is available from the British Library

ISBN 978 1 85856 479 1

Designed and typeset by Trentham Books Ltd, Chester and printed in Great Britain by Page Bros (Norwich) Ltd, Norfolk

Cover photograph by Emma Hertzberg for the British Association for Early Childhood Education.

This publication was first developed as part of the Effective Provision of Pre-school Education (EPPE) project. This longitudinal study funded by the UK Government has followed the development of a large sample of children from 3 years to age 16 (see Department for Children, School and Families research at http://www.dcsf.gov.uk/research). The ECERS-E was first published by Trentham Books in 2003. For information on EPPE, EPPE 3-11, EPPSE 3-14 and EPPSE 16+ visit http://eppe.ioe.ac.uk

Principal Investigators of the EPPE Research Project

Professor Kathy Sylva
Department of Education, University of Oxford

Professor Edward Melhuish
Institute for the Study of Children, Families and Social Issues, Birkbeck, University of London

Professor Pam Sammons
Department of Education, University of Oxford

Professor Iram Siraj-Blatchford
Institute of Education, University of London

Brenda Taggart
Institute of Education, University of London

Acknowledgements

Many people have contributed to the development and testing of this instrument and they have been acknowledged in earlier editions. For the development of this third edition we are indebted to Sandra Mathers and Faye Linskey of A+ Education Ltd. (www.aplus-education.co.uk). Through their training courses with advisory and practitioner groups, as well as their work in assisting UK Local Authorities to use the ECERS for measuring and improving quality, they have become experts on the scales. We have benefitted from their expertise in expanding the notes for clarification. This has been done by listening to the views of those who work every day with young children, collected from hundreds of field visits. Sandra and Faye have a unique and powerful blend of research experience coupled with practitioner knowledge. They will continue to be involved with the scales by developing the All About ECERS-E. We are grateful to them both for their diligence, fine attention to detail and most importantly, their imaginative approach to assessment.

Contents

Foreword

With the increased emphasis on school readiness, it has become extremely important to ensure that the teaching approaches used with young children to promote literacy, mathematics and science resist the tendency to become rigid and academically inappropriate. Recognising that high quality pre-school settings must provide pre-school age children with developmentally appropriate activities to introduce the basic skills that prepare them for success in school, the authors of the ECERS-E expanded several items in the ECERS-R, with the approval of the ECERS-R authors, into complete subscales, as an 'extension' to be used with the ECERS – hence the title ECERS-E. The ECERS-R items expanded into these supplementary subscales include the four Language-Reasoning items, as well as the Math/number, Nature/science, and Promoting acceptance of diversity items. The ECERS-E was used along with the ECERS-R in the Effective Provision of Pre-school Education (EPPE) Project in England (1997-2003). The ECERS-E was published in 2003 as a research edition, and revised in 2006. The current edition provides further revisions and expanded notes and is intended for a wide audience outside the research community.

The authors of the ECERS-E are highly respected in the Early Childhood field. They are also valued colleagues of ours, and long time users of the ECERS. At every step of the way, they have shared their work with us and with many others who use the ECERS for research in different countries. The resulting ECERS-E, which consists of four curricular subscales, is completely in keeping with both the format and the educational philosophy of the ECERS. The authors of the ECERS-E have continued to use their instrument along with the ECERS-R, as have many of their colleagues in the US and in other countries, both for research and programme improvement.

We are pleased that the ECERS-E will now be more widely available for use as an extension to the ECERS-R. We welcome this addition to the ECERS family of assessment instruments, and are hopeful that together they will continue to guide all those who work with young children to provide productive and engaging learning environments in which children flourish.

Professor Thelma Harms
Lead author of Early Childhood Environment Rating Scale-Revised
University of North Carolina at Chapel Hill
2009

Introduction to the ECERS-E

The original Environment Rating Scales were developed in the US by Thelma Harms, Dick Clifford and Debby Cryer of the Frank Porter Graham Child Development Institute at the University of North Carolina. This curricular extension to the ECERS-R or the ECERS-E as it has become known, belongs to a 'family' of scales developed to assess provision for children aged 0 to 12 years. The 'family' includes

- *The Infant/Toddler Environment Rating Scale (ITERS-R*)* designed to assess group programmes for children from birth to 2 $^1/_2$ years of age (Harms, Clifford and Cryer, 2003)
- *The Early Childhood Environment Rating Scale (ECERS-R*)* which assesses centre-based provision for children between the age of 2 $^1/_2$ to 5 years (Harms, Clifford and Cryer, 1998)
- *The School-Age Care Environment Rating Scale (SACERS)* to assess group-care for children of school age, 5 – 12 years (Harms, Jacobs and White, 1996) and
- *The Family Child Care Environment Rating Scale (FCCERS-R*)* designed to assess family child-care programmes conducted in a provider's home for children from infancy through school age (Harms, Cryer and Clifford, 2007).

* R indicates Revised.
For more information on the family of ECERS visit: http://www.fpg.unc.edu/~ECERS/

The American *Early Childhood Environment Rating Scale – Revised* (Harms, Clifford and Cryer, 1998) is a highly respected tool for research, self evaluation, audit and inspection. It is used extensively in the US for both state-wide audits to monitor quality of provision and the training of early years practitioners. Its international reputation is impressive; it has been used in more than twenty countries – from Singapore to Chile. It has been translated and used extensively in Germany (Tietze *et al*, 1996), in the United Kingdom (Sylva *et al*, 1999) and in India (Tamil Nadu) and China (Beijing) researchers such as Islay (2000) and Yan Yan (2008) have used the ECERS as a conceptual template on which to build a very different assessment system to suit environments and practices which are far removed from the American Early Childhood settings in which ECERS was first developed.

ECERS-E: The Early Childhood Environment Rating Scale Curricular Extension to ECERS-R was first developed for use in the Effective Provision of Pre-school Education (EPPE) project which ran from 1997 to 2003. This longitudinal study, funded by the UK Government (see http://eppe.ioe.ac.uk), needed measures of pre-school quality which were rigorous for research and also had credibility with the practitioner community. The adoption of the American ECERS-R was uncontested but the EPPE team needed to extend this into contexts more suited to England's developing frameworks for early years education and care. The ECERS-R was developed in the 1980s, based broadly on notions of Developmentally Appropriate Practice (DAP). It adopted a light touch to assessing provision for developing children's emerging literacy, numeracy and scientific thinking. Moreover, it is also light on assessing provision aimed at cultural and intellectual diversity in the setting. The ECERS-E sought to supplement the ECERS-R in ways that reflected the *English Curriculum Guidance for the Foundation Stage* (QCA, 2000) as well as the changing notions of Developmentally Appropriate Practice, especially as these relate to emerging literacy, numeracy, scientific thinking and diversity.

The ECERS-E assesses provision for children aged 3 to 5 years in the following areas:

■ Literacy
■ Mathematics
■ Science/environment
■ Diversity (Race, Gender and Individual Learning Needs).

The items in these subscales assess the quality of curricular provision, including pedagogy, in these domains aimed at fostering children's academic development (Sammons *et al*, 2002).

The analyses of the EPPE data (which followed the progress and development of approximately 3,000 children from 3 to 11 – see Sylva *et al*, 2004 and Sylva *et al*, 2008) revealed the ECERS-E as a better predictor of children's intellectual and language progress (3-5 years) than assessments on the same settings using the ECERS-R.

The predictive validity of the ECERS-R was compared to this extension (ECERS-E) relying on the same format but with more detailed assessment of the 'curricular environment' which is specified in the *English Foundation Stage Curriculum Guidance*, QCA (2000). Scores on the total ECERS-R were not related to cognitive progress over the two year period but the scores on one of its subscales 'Social Interaction' were positively related to increases in children's **independence** and **cooperation**.

For academic development, however, the ECERS-E was significantly related to progress in children's **language**, **non-verbal reasoning**, **number skills** and **pre-reading skills**. We suggest that quality is not a universal concept but depends on national priorities. If academic achievement is valued at the start of school, then the ECERS-E is a good predictor of readiness for school. But if social outcomes are valued, then the social interaction scale on the ECERS-R may be a better predictor of readiness. However, we strongly believe both are equally important and therefore recommend that the scales should be used together. This is particularly important when using ECERS to monitor quality across a range of different frameworks. ECERS resonates well with many of the domains included in inspections carried out by the Office for Standards in Education (Ofsted), the English regulatory body responsible for the inspection of pre-schools and schools. When preparing for an Ofsted inspection, centre managers and their staff have found both the ECERS-R and the ECERS-E useful in preparing the Self Assessment Form. In the current version of the SEF (Ofsted, 2008) for example, the ECERS is particularly relevant to the following sections:

Part B: **Section 3 – the learning and development of the children in the early years provision**

- Support learning in interactions with children
- Planning the learning environment to help children progress towards the early learning goals
- Plan children's play with a balance of adult-led and child-led activities to help children think critically and be active and creative learners
- Plan for individual needs

Section 4 – the welfare of children in the early years provision

- Helping children to develop skills for the future
- How effective is the setting's self evaluation, including the steps taken to promote improvements?
- How effectively is the provision in the Early Years Foundation Stage led and managed?

Section 6 – the overall effectiveness of the early years provision

- How does the setting maintain continuous improvement?

The authors recognise that the specific format of the SEF may change but the broad areas outlined above will remain relevant to all those involved in self evaluation.

The ECERS-E and ECERS-R have been used extensively over the last ten years as reliable and credible measures of quality in UK research. They have been used in the UK on the following high profile studies (as well as a number of smaller research projects):

The Effective Pre-school Provision in Northern Ireland (EPPNI) – http://www.deni.gov.uk/researchreport41-2.pdf

The Millennium Cohort Study (MCS) – http://www.cls.ioe.ac.uk/studies.asp?section=000100020001

The National Evaluation of the Neighbourhood Nurseries Initiative http://www.dcsf.gov.uk/research/data/uploadfiles/SSU2007FR024.pdf

The National Evaluation of Sure Start http://www.ness.bbk.ac.uk/

The Monitoring and Evaluation of the Effective Implementation of the Foundation Phase (MEEIFP) Project Across Wales www.327matters.org/Docs/meeifp.pdf

Evaluation of the Early Education Pilot for Two Year Old Children (2006-2009) http://www.dcsf.gov.uk/research/data/uploadfiles/DCSF-RR134.pdf

Evaluation of the Graduate Leader Fund (2007-2011) http://www.education.ox.ac.uk/research/resgroup/fell/cfellrp.php

Understanding the nature of the ECERS-E

The ECERS-E was published in 2003 as a 'research edition'. Our goal was to share supplementary material providing more fine-grained assessment of curriculum and pedagogy in early childhood settings with researchers in the UK and elsewhere who were using ECERS-R.

When the ECERS-E was originally developed, it was being used by a team of researchers who knew the scale and its aims very well. No additional notes and clarifications were provided for the items and indicators because the people using it understood their intent and how each should be interpreted. However, now that the scales are being more widely used, it has become necessary to provide additional notes and clarification to support users in applying the scale consistently and appropriately. As questions were received by the authors and those training on the scales, additional clarifications were developed for each item in the scale in response. These notes have improved the consistent use of the scale, but it is important to understand that the notes are intended to support the professional judgement of observers and not to constrain them.

ECERS-E and assessing pedagogy – the 'spirit' of the scale

Although the individual subscales bear the titles of curriculum areas such as 'Mathematics', the quality ratings within each item are tuned to pedagogy and resources as well as to curriculum. Across the four subscales, each item is scored with reference to pedagogy, resources and the setting's organisation. Discrete indicators usually focus on one of these at a time.

Settings which score well on the ECERS-E will be those in which there is a balance of child- and adult-initiated activity and a good deal of 'sustained shared thinking' based on a pedagogy of co-construction (Siraj-Blatchford, Sylva, Muttock, Gilden and Bell, DfES Research Report, 2002). Credit is also given across all four subscales for evidence of planning and child assessment, according to children's individual needs and interests.

- Many of the items are scored 3 if the pedagogy seems 'accidental' or lacks coherence.
- A score of 5 is given if the setting shows evidence of adult guidance balanced with child play and/or exploration.
- A score of 7 is reserved for pedagogy in which adult and child both contribute to the construction of shared meanings, knowledge and skills.

Materials and resources are scored in the same way, with a 3 given for limited although appropriate materials, a 5 given to a wider array of materials and a 7 reserved for resources suited to the active use of materials by children of differing capabilities, cultural backgrounds and interests.

Cautions in use

The ECERS-R was developed as a tool for research, but also as a tool to guide practice. In contrast, the ECERS-E was originally developed for research purposes. It was created as part of the EPPE project as an extension to the ECERS-R, in order to ensure greater depth and rigour in certain areas, specifically in the domains aimed at fostering children's emerging literacy, numeracy and scientific thinking. The ECERS-E is now also widely used as a tool for quality improvement, and can offer valuable guidance in this regard. However, it is important for a number of reasons to remember the context in which the scale was developed:

1   The ECERS-E was designed as an extension to the ECERS-R, rather than as a stand-alone tool, and it is important that it is not presented or used as such. It focuses on certain aspects of curricular provision (i.e. literacy, maths, science/environment and diversity) while not addressing others (e.g. creativity, Personal, Social Education, ICT). The fact that these other aspects of provision are not addressed by the ECERS-E does not mean that they are less important than literacy, maths and science, but simply reflect that they were not the focus of the EPPE project. Presenting the ECERS-E as a stand-alone tool may give the impression that the areas addressed are more important than other areas of provision not addressed (i.e. creativity, PSE, ICT) but this is not the authors' intention. When used alongside the ECERS-R as intended, ECERS-E adds greater depth to certain areas.

2   The ECERS-E was designed to assess quality rather than as a specific professional development tool. Accordingly, the items of the scale do not provide a comprehensive series of steps to work through in developing quality within a particular area. Rather, they contain a series of 'indicators' of quality at each level. For example, the indicators representing 7 (excellent) within the item 'Emergent writing/mark making' are examples of the kinds of provision one might see in excellent settings. However, they do not necessarily include every single requirement one would expect in a high quality environment. It is important that settings do not adopt a 'tick box' approach and seek to address the requirements listed in the ECERS-E to the exclusion of other improvements simply because they are the ones which are listed. This would not be in the 'spirit' of the scales.

3   As stated above, the ECERS cannot cover all aspects of pre-school practice, neither does it provide universal coverage within subscales. Settings which score at 7 (excellent) across the board will still need to consider their developmental needs – there is always room for improvement.

4   Settings which have successfully used ECERS-R and ECERS-E for critically evaluating their own provision and practices have found them particularly useful as tools to open up debate amongst their practitioners about what constitutes 'quality'. Having this debate before embarking on the administration of the scales can lead to a more supportive culture in which to make changes, and a deeper understanding of quality. During training sessions practitioners have often commented on how they value working 'with the scales' as opposed to having 'ECERS done to them' (see **Using ECERS as a self assessment and improvement tool** page 20).

Terminology

It is useful to note that the broad headings Literacy, Mathematics, Science etc. are referred to as SUBSCALES. Each subheading within a SUBSCALE is referred to as an ITEM and each text block within the ITEM is referred to as an INDICATOR. For example:

SUBSCALE= Literacy

ITEM = Print in the environment

INDICATOR 1.1 No labelled pictures are visible to the children.

Throughout the scale, the word 'staff' is used as a generic term to cover all adults who work regularly with children in the setting being observed. This could include volunteers and/or trainees/students as well as paid staff members.

When resources are described as 'accessible' it means that children can get to them unassisted and for a substantial part of the day.

Before using the scales

Before using the ECERS-E scale as either a self-assessment tool (see next section) or research instrument, users are strongly recommended to make themselves familiar with the ECERS-R scale. The Teachers College Press have produced a range of materials to accompany the ECERS-R for training purposes. These include video extracts and advice on making judgements. These materials can be used for both group and self-instruction. After viewing the training package, users will need to conduct several 'trial' observations in order to familiarise themselves with the content of the items included in the scale. This cannot be done in a single observation.

Using the scales demands a high degree of understanding about not only the content of the scales but also making sense of what is being observed. In many cases information to complete the scales cannot be readily observed and the user will need to question the staff sensitively about their practices. Any user therefore needs to be familiar with the content of the scales and also to be confident about probing for additional information beyond that which is observed. Having a background grounded in early years practice and good understanding of appropriate early years practice and child development will be an asset in making judgements in early years settings.

Before using the scales, users should note that it is STRONGLY recommended that users/observers have some external training and validation conducted on their judgements. This could be done by a colleague or outsider as a measure of inter-rater reliability.

Using the ECERS-E

Preparing for the observation

- As with the other Environment Rating Scales, the ECERS-E is designed to be used with one group of children at a time. All areas to which the group of children have access should be observed.

- Sufficient time should be allocated to conduct the observations. At least 3 or 4 hours should be set aside to complete the ECERS-E. However, longer may be needed to see the range of activities assessed, and to gain an accurate picture of provision. It is recommended that you observe for at least six hours (for example from 9 am to 3 pm).

- If you are using both the ECERS-R and the ECERS-E, you may want to complete the ECERS-R after the first few hours (the authors of the ECERS-R recommend an observation time of 3 to 4 hours) and then carry on observing to gather more evidence for the ECERS-E.

- You will need some time at the end of the observation to talk with a member of staff and ask any additional questions. This should be at a time when the member of staff is free from childcare responsibilities. You will also need to have access to paperwork such as planning and child observations/records, and may need to allow a little extra time to ask questions about these if necessary. It is advisable to let the setting know before your visit that you will be asking to see documentation. Allow sufficient time for staff to get this for you.

- Before beginning the observation, ensure you have completed as much of the identifying information as possible: the name of the centre, age group observed etc.

- Spend some time before the observation familiarising yourself with the centre and its geography. It is a good idea to find out from the staff what activities are planned during the period of the observation.

- Make sure that you are clear about the definitions of the terms used throughout the scale. For example, 'a few' (Print in the environment 3.1) suggests a limited number, probably no more than 5, while 'many' (same item 5.1) suggests more than 5. Clear distinctions (% value) should be made between 'few', 'some', 'many', 'variety', 'most', 'sometimes' and agreed by the observer and inter-rater. In this context 'easily accessible' pertaining to books and literacy areas means that children can reach and use materials easily, not necessarily that every child has to have access to all of them at all times. The term 'staff' refers to all adults who have direct contact with children.

Conducting the observation

1   The items do not have to be completed in the order in which they appear in the book. If a cooking activity is taking place you may decide to score this immediately and then come back to other items later. Some items may be scored more easily than others.

2   Only score an item after you have allowed sufficient time to make a reasoned judgement. This is particularly important for items which demand observing the interactions between adult/child or child/child. You need to be sure that what you are observing is representative of the practices as a whole.

3   Take care not to interrupt the activities being observed. The observer should be like a 'fly on the wall' and should avoid interacting with the children or staff. It is important to be as unobtrusive as possible and to remain neutral in your actions, expressions and replies to questions.

4   If you are unsure about something, make detailed notes on your scoring sheet and ensure they are clear enough for you to follow when you come back to them at the end of the observation to discuss them with a critical friend in order to make a sound judgement. This is particularly important if you are using the scales for self-evaluation and plan to give feedback to others on your observations.

5   Make sure you score all items at the time of the observation. It is very difficult to record scores away from the setting.

6   A new score sheet should be used for each observation (permission is granted to photocopy score sheets only) and you should make sure the scoring is both legible and photocopiable. It is recommended that you use a pencil and have a eraser with you to amend scoring as you work.

Scoring the scales

Scoring should only be completed once the observer is familiar with the scale. Read the items carefully, as it is essential that judgements are made exactly in accordance with the instructions given.

1   Scores must reflect the observed practice and not some future plan the staff may have told you about.

2   The scale measures from 1 to 7 with 1 = inadequate, 3 = minimal, 5 = good and 7 = excellent.

3   The observation should always start with 1 and be worked though systematically.

4   A rating of 1 must be given if **any** indicator in section 1 is scored YES.

5   A rating of 2 is given when **all** indicators under 1 are scored NO and at least half of the indicators under 3 are scored YES.

6   A rating of 3 is given when **all** indicators under 1 scored NO and **all** indictors under 3 are scored YES.

7   A rating of 4 is given when **all** indicators under 3 are met and at least half of the indicators under 5 are scored YES.

8   A rating of 5 is given when **all** indicators under 5 are scored YES.

9   A rating of 6 is given when **all** indicators under 5 are met and at least half of the indicators under 7 are scored YES.

10 A rating of 7 is given when **all** indicators under 7 are scored YES.

11 A score of NA (Not Applicable) may only be given for entire items where there are options e.g. 9a Shape or 9b Sorting, matching and comparing. These items have an NA option on the score sheet.

12 To calculate average subscale scores, add up the scores for each item in the subscale and divide by the number of items scored. The total mean scale score is the sum of all item scores for the entire scale, divided by the number of items scored.

NB. These administrative notes are based on the ECERS-R guidance. We are grateful to the Chapel Hill Team for their assistance in helping us write our guidance notes.

Optional Scoring Systems

Unlike the ECERS-R, the ECERS-E has some optional items. As ECERS-E focuses on opportunities to provide learning experiences, there may however be activities which are not evident during the observations but which cover important aspects of curriculum provision. Before choosing which of the optional items to assess, look carefully at the range of activities on offer during the observation period to see which item you have the most evidence for scoring. If in doubt you can score all items, including the optional ones and make a judgement on which optional items most accurately reflect children's overall experiences in that curriculum area.

Some items in the maths and science subscales are optional. The first two maths items are always scored. The observer should select either 'Shape' or 'Sorting, matching and comparing'.

The first two science items are always scored. The observer should then select either 'Non-living' or 'Living processes and the world around us' or 'Food preparation'.

The idea behind the optional system is to make the observation manageable for settings. The ECERS-E assesses complex pedagogical interactions and it would be impossible to expect to see all the behaviours and activities listed during an observation. The optional item system allows us to give credit for what is most evident on the observation day.

For example, the three optional science items assess the same concepts (e.g. where staff are encouraging children to use different senses to explore and talk about their experiences) but across different domains of science – 'Non-living', 'Living processes and the world around us' and 'Food preparation'. Usually, we would not decide which of these areas to score until later in the observation. It is good practice to gather evidence for all optional items and then decide at the end which scored most highly. For example, if you see a baking activity you might have gathered most evidence for 'Food preparation'. In this case you would complete the scoring for this item and cross through the other two optional science items. In this way, you can give the setting credit for their best practice on the day.

In terms of scoring you would always submit three item scores for 'Science' – Items 1, 2 and then whichever of the optional items you choose. If practitioners are using the scales in a more developmental way (e.g. over time to support improvements in practice), then they might want to use all of the optional items.

Use of supplementary (non-observation) evidence

Since the ECERS-E is an observational scale, the majority of activities and behaviours will need to be observed to give credit. In some cases, supplementary evidence can be used, for example display or children's records/portfolios. Where it is appropriate to supplement observation with evidence from other sources, individual items are marked as follows:

- P – evidence from planning acceptable
- D – evidence from displays/photographic records acceptable
- R – evidence from children's records acceptable (includes children's portfolios or folders of completed work)
- Q – evidence from questioning acceptable.

NB. These are also marked on the score sheet next to the relevant indicators. When scoring, these letters can be circled to show which source of evidence has been used.

Throughout the scale, indicators for which evidence other than observations can be used are marked accordingly (using P, D, R and/or Q). A small number of these relate specifically to planning and/or records and require evidence to be present in these forms. For example, the following indicator from the Science subscale requires that the introduction of scientific concepts needs to be planned for. In this case evidence is <u>required</u>:

5.1 Staff often plan and introduce appropriate scientific concepts (e.g. how materials change, magnetism, sinkers and floaters) and children handle materials. *P, D, R

However, for most of the items which allow evidence from supplementary sources, these additional sources of evidence should only be sought when 'observable' examples are lacking. Observation always provides the best evidence since there is no way of knowing how well a particular activity was carried out when using evidence from display or records (or, in the case of planning evidence, whether in fact the activity was carried out at all). For example in the following indicator from the Science subscale, credit can be given if this is observed on the day. If no examples are directly observed, evidence from planning and/or display can be used:

5.1 Natural materials are used beyond decoration to illustrate specific concepts, e.g. planting seeds or bulbs to demonstrate growth. P D *

Do not give credit for activities shown in the planning where your observations on the day do not support the planning evidence.

In some cases, evidence from planning, records and/or display can only be used as <u>supporting</u> evidence and a particular activity must also be observed to give credit. In these cases, the P, D and R are shown in brackets:

7.1 Children are encouraged to identify and explore a range of natural phenomena in their environment outside the centre and talk about/describe them. (P, D)*

The notes for this indicator make it clear that at least one discussion relating to nature/natural materials should be observed. Planning or display evidence can then be used as supporting evidence that children experience a range of natural phenomena.

How much evidence to review?
When using the ECERS-E for assessment or audit, we suggest that the observer reviews a sample of paper-based evidence:

- Long, medium and short term planning for progress (or at least the most recent plans, possibly covering the previous six weeks if these are fairly typical)*
- Records (e.g. learning stories, portfolios of work) kept on three children. If possible, records should show a range of ages/stages, for example one child who is ahead of the group in one or more areas, a child in mid-range, and a child who struggles in one or more areas
- Paperwork relating to at least one child with additional or special needs (e.g. Individual Education Plan) if applicable
- The display currently in the room (e.g. photos of recent activities, books prepared for parents to show recent activities carried out by the group, display boards of children's work). As a general guide, if display is used as evidence this should be no more than six to eight weeks old.

NB: It is also advisable to ask a member of staff to talk you through the planning and record-keeping process.

* Some evidence of planning for progress should be available for approximately the past six typical weeks. It is recognised that short term planning will be in response to children's interests and needs and cannot be completed much in advance whereas medium term planning around, for example, continuous provision areas, possible themes and seasonal enhancements should reflect the work of the setting and be available. Long term objectives and both short and longitudinal planning should be documented in some way.

Throughout the scale, where evidence from planning, records or display is acceptable, guidelines are suggested as to how many examples should be seen within the evidence reviewed. But these guidelines are not hard and fast, as every setting plans and records evidence in a different way. Observers should also use their judgment about whether a particular activity or concept is adequately provided for. Where the ECERS-E is being used in a more developmental way (e.g. by a staff team over time), it is useful to consider more than a six week period of planning, and to review children's records more comprehensively.

Using ECERS as a self assessment and improvement tool

ECERS-R and ECERS-E can be used in settings for not only improving practice but also providing evidence of

- self evaluation,
- reflective practice and
- development planning

at both Centre level and Local Authority level.

Improvement at centre level

Since the publication of the Effective Provision of Pre-School Education (EPPE) Technical Papers which relate quality, as measured by ECERS-R and ECERS-E, with child cognitive and social/behavioural developmental outcomes for children aged 3-5, we have been inundated with requests for the ECERS-E document (which was particularly significant for cognitive outcomes – see Introduction) not only within the UK but also from around the world. We have asked people what they wanted the scale for and most replied that they want to use it in their early childhood settings for self-assessment or as a research instrument.

We discussed, as a team, what it means for people to use the scales when they haven't been trained to do so. We are concerned about their use in settings where the general professional training of the staff may be limited. We are certain that in such circumstances critical but constructive support will be needed. We also worry about the lack of external validation or external moderation, which allows settings to rate themselves as good, excellent or in need of further development, but with no real comparative measure.

Because of these concerns we used the ECERS-R and ECERS-E as part of the three year long Early Excellence Evaluations of two centres: Gamesley Early Excellence Centre in Derbyshire and the Thomas Coram Early Excellence Centre in London (Siraj-Blatchford, 2002a and 2002b). With the support of their heads and senior teachers, the centres used the ECERS-R and ECERS-E scales as a self-development tool.

All the staff first received a full day's training on the meaning of 'quality' – both the culturally specific aspects and what we consider universal aspects such as treating children with respect, not smacking or harming children. The staff were introduced to the ECERS-R and the ECERS-E and trained by a trained researcher/user of the scales, using the ECERS-R video and Guide produced by Teachers College Press.

The staff were given time to compare and discuss their judgements and then asked to trial two of the scales for themselves, working in pairs. In a follow-up half day session they reported back their findings, also their agreements and disagreements.

During the three years, the staff regularly reported on their discussions and progress with the scales. They found it easier to begin by rating the less threatening subscales, such as furnishings and display. From this they learnt that it was the actual discussions that generated the most useful outcomes. These discussions led them to agree meanings for good practice. The staff recommended that each rater should discuss their ratings, which they undertook independently but based on the same observations, immediately afterwards, compare their ratings and discuss why their perceptions sometimes differed. As the staff became more confident about their ratings and discussions they became more critical of the setting and their practices, and at times also more critical about aspects of the scales. All this was perceived as productive, as most of their observations led to positive actions. For instance the Thomas Coram EEC, after rating their 'Language and Reasoning' subscale, decided to take the following action:

within six months to:

■ provide in-service training for all staff on extending children's conversations, focusing on developing the use of open-ended questions

■ establish listening areas in the rooms used by children aged 3 – 5.

within a year:

■ to order more dressing-up clothes and to increase the range and quality of the clothes for socio-dramatic play.

Similarly, after the staff at the Gamesley FEC had rated the ECERS-R subscale on Personal Care Routines, they made a decision on the item 'Greetings and departures'. Although staff felt that greeting the parents and children at the nursery was well organised, some were concerned because the departure in the afternoon meant that some children missed out on the important story session. The staff also felt there was too little time to talk or share information with the parents.

> '*All very rushed*, parents also have to hunt for their children, as each nursery officer went into a different room for small group/ story time' (Lynn Kennington, Head teacher, Gamesley EEC).

There was intense discussion amongst the staff about how they could improve departure time.

Action taken: The arrival and departure time for children who attended nursery in the afternoon was changed. The session had begun at 12.45pm and finished at 3.15pm. Now, instead of going into small groups for story time, all the nursery groups join together for a large group story. The staff, on a rota basis, read the story and the parents collect their children from this group. This helped parents know where they can find their children and gave the nursery officers who are not reading the story time to share information with parents about their child. The result was that the story sessions were no longer interrupted and there were opportunities for staff and parents to discuss matters regarding their children.

Both centres documented and discussed examples from the ECERS-R and ECER-E. They agreed certain actions and carried them out. They closely monitored the changes made and the outcomes were recorded and revisited. This developmental work allowed staff to reflect, plan and monitor the children's welfare and learning. It became an integral part of the ongoing centre development plans and policies in both centres.

After two years of such development, the centre heads agreed to take part in an external validation exercise where another trained researcher who had no prior knowledge of it came into their centre, and rated it for its environmental quality, using both the ECERS-R and ECERS-E. Both centres scored an average of six on both scales, placing them between good and excellent on both. They are continuing to use the scales and are also looking at ITERS (Infant and Toddler Environmental Rating Scale) to engage in self-assessment and the development of their practice with the children who are under three years old.

What has been learnt from this experience? When interviewed as part of their annual evaluation, both headteachers made it clear that they had taken the exercise very seriously. When asked why they undertook this trial in their centre, Bernadette Duffy, Head of Thomas Coram and Coram Parents' Early Excellence Centre replied: *'It's about being brave enough to be objective, it's about being self-critical and hard on yourself'*.

Lynn Kennington, Head of Gamesley Early Excellence Centre said: *'The discussion process is the best, we got quite high scores but we could be doing better than even what's measured, we as staff are not entirely happy with this and feel we could go further'*.

Clearly then, the ECERS can be used effectively as a self-assessment and improvement tool at pre-school centres and reception class level (first year of compulsory schooling) as long as the following criteria are met:

- that rigorous training is provided on both the quality criteria (definitions and cultural variations) and on the use and the role of the scales
- that it is recognised that an exercise of this nature requires a critical mass of reflective practitioners within the setting
- that a critical friend supports the initiative (an insider e.g. local authority adviser or a representative from Higher Education. In the cases of Gamesley and Thomas Coram centres, their external evaluator also acted as critical friend).
- that there is willingness to undergo external validation in the form of 'blind' assessment by a trained, reliable assessor.

We are grateful to the staff and the head teachers of Gamesley and Thomas Coram EECs for their time and efforts in using the ECERS instruments and in helping us to understand how they can best be used by centres as a self-assessment tool.

Improvement at Local Authority level

The ECERS-R and ECERS-E can support leaders and practitioners in implementing quality improvement by providing an empowering tool which offers a clear and concrete path for them to follow (see Mathers *et al*, 2007b). This has been particularly important in the UK settings which are inspected under the Office for Standards in Education (Ofsted). Pending an inspection, Leaders of Early Years settings have to provide information on a Self Evaluation Form (SEF), and ECERS has been invaluable in helping settings chart their 'improvement journey'. But the scales can also bring major benefits to Local Authority Early Years Services.

ECERS- R and ECERS-E are cited in the revised *Practice Guidance for the Early Years Foundation Stage* (May 2008, p9) as examples of 'quality improvement tools' and many Local Authorities are now using them for:

- quality improvement and supported self-assessment: a tool for advisers and consultants to work with settings and identify priorities for improvement

- quality assurance: as a QA framework in its own right, or alongside existing schemes

- audits to provide information at authority level: mapping quality trends across the authority to prioritise spending, training and support

- measuring change: e.g. assessing the impact of new initiatives.

One such Authority is Derbyshire, which in 2007 had a population of 40,000 children under five years old (Office of National Statistics, http://www.statistics.gov.uk/default.asp). Derbyshire is working in partnership with settings to complete an audit as a quality improvement tool. Attracted by the international reputation of the scales and the fact that they are mentioned in the EYFS guidance, the Authority is in the first year of a phased roll-out of the scales to its 300 schools and 300 Private, Voluntary and Independent settings. '*We saw the scales as the next step in encouraging reflective practice in our schools and settings, and as a way to build knowledge and confidence among practitioners. They are tools that give settings ... a clear idea of what they are good at, what they need to change and how to get there*' (Sue Ricketts, Senior Adviser, Education Improvement Derbyshire County Council).

Similarly, the Early Years and Childcare Service of Surrey Local Authority, with a population in 2007 of 52,200 children under five (Office of National Statistics), have used ECERS-R and ECERS-E audits to target support and measure improvements in settings as part of an Authority wide audit of its 500 Private, Voluntary and Independent settings. As part of their self-evaluation process, leaders, in consultation with their staff, are expected to use the scales to set targets and put together action plans to improve the quality of provision.

The use of ECERS-R and ECERS-E, whether at Authority or setting level, should be a transparent, inclusive and positive experience that involves and empowers staff and harnesses their enthusiasm for excellent practice.

Item	Inadequate 1	2	Minimal 3	4	Good 5	6	Excellent 7

Literacy

Item 1. Print in the environment (see definition opposite)

1.1 No labelled pictures are visible to the children. * D

1.2 No environmental print which is relevant to children on display.* D

3.1 A few labelled pictures are present and visible to children. * D

3.2 A few labelled objects or items are present and easily visible to the children (*e.g. labels on shelves, children's names on coat pegs or paintings, pots labelled 'pens', 'pencils'*). *

3.3 Printed words are prominently displayed (*e.g. 'welcome' on the door, titles on art displays, labels designating interest centres within the room such as the art area or sand/water area.*) * D

5.1 Many labelled pictures are on view to the children, indicating a print-rich environment. * D

5.2 Children are encouraged to recognise printed words in their environment (*e.g. their own names on peg labels, print on everyday objects such as food packaging or carrier bags*).*

5.3 Children are encouraged to recognise letters in their environment (*e.g. staff draw attention to the individual letters in a child's name, or in other environmental print*). *

7.1 Discussion of environmental print takes place and often relates to objects of personal interest to the children. *

7.2 There is discussion of the relationship between the spoken and the printed word (*e.g. discussing how to read the words written on a child's T-shirt*). *

7.3 Children are encouraged to recognise letters <u>and</u> words in their environment other than their own names (*e.g. in words on labels or posters*).*

Notes for clarification

Environmental print includes all printed words in the child's environment including words that are attached or superimposed on an object that has meaning for the child. To be truly 'environmental' it must have meaning relevant to the object it relates to, for example, storage signs that include a picture and the name of the stored items, labels on shelves/children's pegs, print on packaging/clothing/carrier bags, printed instructions on picture signs ('please wash your hands'). These can be handwritten or printed.

Words which form part of resources (e.g. books, games, flash-cards) are not considered to be 'environmental print' as there is no illustrative meaning attached to the words. Do not count displays or other text that are relevant to adults rather than children.

Labelled pictures (1.1, 3.1, 5.1): Do not count print without pictures. Pictures must be accompanied by brief text relating to the content of the picture (*e.g. a poster of a car with the word 'car' printed below, drawer labels with pictures <u>and</u> text labels to identify the contents*). The text must be in large enough print to be read from a distance, and to be read by the children.

3.1 Two or more different examples.

3.2 Two or more different examples.

3.3 Print may be above eye level but children should be able to see it easily.

5.1 To give credit, at least five or more different examples should be present and easily visible to the children. The observer should be satisfied that the environment is 'print-rich' in order to give credit.

5.2 To give credit, staff should be observed explicitly encouraging children to recognise environmental print (at least one example observed) or the observer should see evidence of a regular daily routine which encourages children to recognise print in the environment (e.g. a self-registration system, where children find their names and post them on a board to show that they are present).

5.3 At least one example should be observed of adults drawing explicit attention to letters .

7.1 Discussions must actively involve children and be more than a passing mention. At least two examples must be observed, one of which must relate to an item clearly of personal interest to the children (e.g. a child's T-shirt, print on postcards sent by other children in the group, print on an object a child has brought in from home).

7.2 Discussion must actively involve children. At least one example should be observed.

7.3 To give credit, observers should see at least one example of staff encouraging children to recognise words in the environment and at least one example of staff encouraging children to recognise letters.

Item	Inadequate 1	2	Minimal 3	4	Good 5	6	Excellent 7

Item 2. Book and literacy areas

1.1 Books are unattractive. *

1.2 Books are not of a suitable age level.*

3.1 Some books of different kinds are accessible to children. *

3.2 An easily accessible area of the room is set aside for books.*

3.3 Some reading takes place in the book area. *

5.1 A variety of types of book is accessible to children. *

5.2 Book area used independently by children.*

7.1 Book area is comfortable (rug and cushions or comfortable seating) and filled with a wide range of books of varied style, content and complexity. *

7.2 Adults encourage children to use books and direct them to the book area.*

7.3 Books are included in learning areas outside the book corner.*

Notes for clarification

1.1   This refers to the books themselves and not the way in which they are displayed. Score yes if 50% or more of the books are damaged.

1.2   Score yes if 50% or more of the books are of an unsuitable age level.

3.1   Possible categories include: picture/story books, reference/information books, poetry/nursery rhymes and counting/maths books. Not all categories are required, but at least three or four examples from two different categories should be accessible to children daily.

3.2   The book area may also be used for other quiet activities and/or for whole group time at certain times of the day, but must generally be intended for the purposeful reading of books.

3.3   This could be during whole group time or informally, by groups or individual children, with or without adults. This indicator is specifically concerned with how extensively the book area (or areas) are used. Do not give credit if books are taken from the book area and used elsewhere (e.g. children select books from the book corner to read at the table while waiting for snack).

5.1   See 3.1 for possible categories of books. Books can be commercially produced or home-made. At least three examples from each category should be accessible to children daily (and observers should also base their decision on the size of the group being catered for).

In addition, the selection should include many books with text, and some variation in the level of books available to cater for different skills (e.g. some simpler and some more complex, dual language texts or books in other languages where the group is diverse).

5.2   At least two (different) examples must be observed. However, when determining whether children regularly access the book area independently of adults, observers should also base their judgement on the size of the group. Children must be accessing the book area for the purpose of selecting and reading books rather than for any other activity.

7.1   In addition to the variety of types required for 5.1, this indicator requires variety within the types of book offered to cater for a range of interests (e.g. information books about science topics, transport topics and different cultures/religions; story books about animals, people and imaginary creatures). Sizes and formats should vary. A greater variation in developmental level is also required than is necessary at 5.1. The area should contain books at many different levels, ranging from simple board books and books with many pictures/little text, to more complex books with a lot of text on each page and other more complex features (e.g. reference books with diagrams).

7.2   This should be observed at least once.

7.3   Books should be provided in at least two other areas to give credit and should have some connection to the learning/play experiences provided in that area (e.g. counting books in the maths area).

Item	Inadequate 1	2	Minimal 3	4	Good 5	6	Excellent 7

Item 3. Adult reading with the children

1.1 Adults rarely read to the children. * P, Q

3.1 Adults read with children daily. * P, Q

3.2 There is some involvement of the children during reading times (*e.g. children are encouraged to join in with repeated words and phrases in the text; adult shares pictures with the child/ren or asks simple questions*).*

5.1 Children take an active role during reading times, and the words and / or story are usually discussed. *

5.2 Children are encouraged to use conjecture, and/or link the content of the book to other experiences. *

7.1 There is discussion about print and letters as well as content.*

7.2 There is support material for the children to engage with stories by themselves (*e.g. tapes, interactive displays, puppets, story sacks, computer games*). D

7.3 There is evidence of one to one reading with some children.*

Notes for clarification

1. 1 Score yes if no reading with the children is seen during the observation and there is no daily reading time listed on the schedule.

3.1 Give credit if two or more examples of informal reading with groups or individual children are seen during the observation. Alternatively, credit can be given if there is evidence of a planned daily reading time which includes all (or most of) the children even if this happens outside the observation time. This could be whole group reading, or planned small group reading times.

3.2 Reading with children must be observed on at least one occasion in order to score this indicator. If several reading times are observed, involvement of children should be a feature of the majority of sessions in order to give credit.

5.1 This must be observed at least once. If several reading sessions are observed, this should be true for most sessions.

5.2 Examples might include an adult asking: '*What do you think [the character] will do next?' or (when reading a factual book about pets) 'Have any of you got a pet at home? How do you take care of them'*. If several reading sessions are observed, this should be true for most sessions.

7.1 This should be observed at least once to give credit.

7.3 Several examples should be observed. It should be clear that informal reading with individual children is a regular part of the daily routine.

Item	Inadequate		Minimal		Good		Excellent
	1	2	3	4	5	6	7

Item 4. Sounds in words

1.1 Few or no rhymes or poems are spoken or sung. * P, Q

3.1 Rhymes are often spoken or sung by adults to children.* P, Q

3.2 Children are encouraged to speak and/or sing rhymes. *

5.1 The rhyming components of songs/rhymes are brought to the attention of children.*

5.2 The initial sounds in words are brought to the attention of children.*

7.1 Attention is paid to syllabification of words (e.g. through *clapping games, jumping etc.*). *P

7.2 Some attention is given to linking sounds to letters. * (P)

Notes for clarification

Rhymes could include nursery rhymes and rhyming songs, poems, rhyming games played on the computer, card games which involve rhymes, rhyming books, or phonics activities which include rhyme. Give credit for rhymes spoken or sung with small groups of children as well as whole group activities. If songs are used as evidence, credit can only be given if they rhyme. Adults must be actively involved. For example, do not give credit if you see children listening to taped songs/rhymes by themselves.

1.1 Score 'yes' if there is evidence that rhymes are spoken or sung fewer than 2 or 3 times per week (e.g. only one singing time scheduled per week and no evidence of informal singing during the session observed).

3.1 Often means daily. Give credit if there is evidence of a planned daily singing/rhyme session which includes all (or the majority of) the children, even if this occurs outside the observation period. Depending on the number of children attending, this may be carried out in a small group rather than as a whole class activity. If there is no daily group session planned, then at least two examples of informal use of rhyme (e.g. singing, rhyming books) with small groups or individual children should be seen during the observation.

3.2 It is not necessary for adults to draw explicit attention to rhyme to give credit at this level. For example, give credit if it is observed that children usually join in during singing sessions, or when reading a rhyming book.

5.1 At least one example must be observed.

5.2 At least two examples must be observed. Adults must draw explicit attention to the initial sounds in words and say the words out loud. (e.g. drawing attention to the fact that 'bat' and 'ball' start with the same letter, by saying 'can you hear – they both begin with 'b'. Can you think of anything else which starts with the same letter?').

7.1 Give credit if this is seen during the observation. If no examples are observed on the day, then at least two examples should be found in the sample of planning reviewed.

7.2 To give credit, observers should either see two examples of adults linking sounds to letters, or see one example and find two examples in the sample of planning reviewed. Examples might include phonics work which makes the link between letters and sounds explicit, or an adult helping a child to write down a particular spoken word.

Item	Inadequate 1	2	Minimal 3	4	Good 5	6	Excellent 7

Item 5. Emergent writing/mark making *

1.1 There are no materials for children to engage in emergent writing. *

1.2 Children never observe staff writing down what they (the children) say.* D, R

3.1 Children have access to implements for writing (e.g. pencils, felt tips, chalks).*

3.2 Children have access to paper or other resources appropriate to a writing task, (e.g. A4 or telephone pads, chalk boards, small wipeable boards for use with dry wipe markers).*

3.3 Children sometimes observe staff writing down what they (the children) say. * D, R

5.1 A place in the setting is set aside for emergent writing. *

5.2 Children often observe staff writing down what they (the children) say.*

5.3 Children are encouraged to 'have a go' at 'writing' to communicate with others (e.g. home-made books, written menus in the 'café', annotating their own picture).

7.1 As well as pencils and paper, the mark making area has a theme to encourage children to 'write', (e.g. an office).

7.2 Adults draw children's attention to the purpose of writing, (e.g. addressing an envelope, making a shopping list, writing a story). * D, R, (P)

7.3 Children's emergent writing is displayed for others to see.* D

Notes for clarification

'**Emergent**' or '**developing**' writing is young children's own attempts at translating oral language into a written form. In its earliest stages it may appear as lines and squiggles, but if asked the child can usually tell you what they have 'written'. As children become more proficient, evidence of letters or numbers begins to emerge from this seemingly random mark making. Children copying what an adult has written is not classed as emergent writing.

1.1 Score 'yes' if children do not have access to writing materials for at least some portion of the day.

1.2/3.3/5.2 Observers should check displays and children's records/portfolios for evidence of staff writing down children's words (i.e. 'scribing' for children). Examples might include children's art work displayed with their words written as a caption underneath. For indicators 1.2 and 3.3, evidence from records and displays can be used. To give credit at 1.2, one example should be found in the materials reviewed. To give credit at 3.3, two examples are required.

However, since there is no way of knowing whether the writing was actually shared with the child, evidence from records/displays is not adequate to give credit for indicator 5.2. To give credit at this level, observers should see at least one example of an adult scribing children's words.

3.1/3.2 To give credit, at least one mark making option should be available for children to access freely for much of the day (i.e. not restricted to 'writing activities'). Variety in materials/media is considered at indicator 5.1 and credit can be given at this minimal level even if the range of options is limited.

5.1 This must be a designated area (or areas) with suitable materials and space to write – it is not enough for children to have access to writing materials which they then take to any available table. A wider variety of materials to encourage mark making should also be available at this level (e.g. a writing area with pens, pencils, crayons, pads, rulers, calendars and diaries; a role play shop with shopping lists, price tags, catalogues, pencils and pads of paper).

7.2 Examples might include writing connected to role play (e.g. labelling parcels in a Post Office) or children contributing to environmental print (e.g. writing labels for their drawers or for displays). If a purposeful writing activity is not seen on the day, observers should look for evidence that such activities have taken place (e.g. displayed materials). At least 3 examples of purposeful writing should be found in the display and records reviewed. Confirmatory evidence can be sought in the planning. However, since the observer will not know how well planning is (or has been) carried out, credit for this indicator should not be given solely on the basis of planning evidence.

7.3 Do not give credit for writing which is copied or traced from an adult's handwriting.

Item	Inadequate		Minimal		Good		Excellent
	1	2	3	4	5	6	7

Item 6. Talking and listening

1.1 Very little encouragement or opportunity for children to talk to adults.

3.1 Some conversation between adults and children occurs (*e.g. adults talk to the children either individually or as a group about an ongoing activity, ask simple questions, respond to children's comments*).

5.1 Interesting experiences are planned by adults and drawn upon to encourage talk and the sharing of ideas. * (P)

7.1 Adults provide scaffolding for children's conversations with them.*

1.2 Most verbal attention from adults is of a supervisory nature.*

3.2 Children are allowed to talk amongst themselves with some limited adult intervention (*e.g. adults ask closed questions*).

5.2 Children are encouraged to answer questions in a more extended way (requiring more than one word answers). *

7.2 Children are often encouraged to talk to each other in small groups, and adults encourage their peers to listen to them.* P

5.3 Adults regularly create one-to-one opportunities to talk with children by initiating conversations with individuals.*

7.3 Adults regularly use open-ended questions to extend the children's language through talk (*e.g. 'what do you think would happen if....?', 'how did you make.....?'*) *

7.4 Children are encouraged to ask questions. *

Notes for clarification

1.2 Score yes if the majority of adult's talk is related to managing routines, activities or behaviour.

5.1 This indicator assesses the extent to which adults plan for talk. Experiences must have an explicit focus on communication and the sharing of ideas. 'Non-literacy' activities (e.g. science experiments) can be counted if there is a planned and explicit focus on discussion. Examples of appropriate planning might include listing key words or questions for a particular activity, or 'brainstorming' at the beginning of a topic to gather children's ideas. As with all items, planning evidence should be used with caution and at least one planned activity must be observed to assess how effectively adults draw on the experience to encourage children's talk. If this is not the case, credit should not be given.

5.2 Credit can be given here for questions which require longer answers than 'yes' or 'no', but which are not as challenging as those required for indicator 7.3. (e.g. an adult might ask a child 'Which animals are you going to put in the barn?' or 'What are you going to wear for the party tomorrow?'). No specific number of examples is required but observers should hear enough evidence to be sure that such questions occur regularly.

5.3 Several examples should be observed, and conversations with individual children should take place in a variety of contexts e.g. during routines, during adult-led activities, during child-initiated free play. Conversations at this level should be more extensive than is required for indicator 3.1, and involve a number of back-and-forth communications between adult and child.

7.1 Scaffolding provides a 'framework' for children's talk. To give credit, adults should be observed accepting and extending children's verbal contributions in conversation (e.g. child says 'Look, the beans are growing', and the adult responds 'Yes, that's right, they're growing really tall. How tall do you think they will get?'). No specific number of examples is required, but observers should hear enough evidence to be sure that extending children's thinking through questioning or strategic commenting is a regular occurrence.

7.2 The emphasis here is on small groups – do not count whole group discussions/circle times when scoring this indicator. The communication should be more focussed than simply talking while taking part in a play activity. Examples might include children talking about models they have made or recalling a trip outside the centre. If planning is used as evidence, the observer should be satisfied that the talk is likely to be of good quality, and that children are encouraged to listen to each other (i.e. evidence from other observations should support this conclusion).

7.3 No specific number of examples is required but observers should hear enough evidence to be sure that such questions are regularly asked.

7.4 At least one explicit example of encouragement must be observed. In addition, where children do ask questions spontaneously, adults should respond in an encouraging and respectful way (e.g. give the child time to ask the question, respond with interest to the question).

Item	Inadequate		Minimal		Good		Excellent
	1	2	3	4	5	6	7

Mathematics – N.B. Items 7 and 8 MUST be assessed. After assessing Items 7 and 8 you may then select *EITHER* Item 9a or Item 9b for evidence. You may choose the item that is most apparent during the observation. This mathematics subscale may require access to planning documents.

Item 7. Counting and the application of counting

1.1 Children rarely take part in activities or routines where counting is used. * P, D, R, Q

1.2 Very few resources are available to encourage the children to take part in counting activities (e.g. conkers, shells, buttons, counting books, games). *

3.1 A few number activities, counting books, games, songs or rhymes are used with the children. * P, D, R, Q

3.2 Numbers are named as part of daily routines. *

3.3 Maths provision includes a few resources which encourage children to take part in counting activities (e.g. posters featuring numbers, sets of countable objects, counting books, games or other resources) D *

5.1 Number activities such as songs, rhymes, counting books and/or games are often used with the children. * (P) (D) (R)

5.2 Children are encouraged to count objects and to associate the spoken numbers with the numerical concepts.

(e.g. counting the number of children present at registration, counting out six milk cartons for six children, asking a child to count the number of blocks in a tower they have made).*

5.3 Adults use ordinal numbers (1st, 2nd, 3rd ..) when working with the children. *

7.1 All children are actively encouraged to take part in counting objects in a variety of contexts, (e.g. role play, snack time, sharing lego). *

7.2 Activities are planned which encourage one-to-one correspondence both indoors and outdoors (or outside the setting). * P

7.3 Adults incorporate into their planning working with children on specific number activities, (e.g. dice games, dominoes, matching numbers to numbers or numbers to pictures). * P

7.4 There is a well-equipped maths area with number games, countable objects and books. *

Notes for clarification

Number activities could include: counting songs/ rhymes; counting books; counting games; computer/interactive whiteboard programmes which include counting; use of maths resources such as number fans during whole group sessions. Observers should also give credit for incidental counting during play. In theory, any play activity is acceptable if adults make counting an explicit and significant part of the activity (i.e. more than a 'passing mention' of number). Activities should be culturally and developmentally appropriate. For example, rote counting, or use of worksheets with no concrete experiences, cannot be counted as evidence of number activities.

Daily routines are non-play based and might include snack or lunchtime, registration, putting coats on and lining up to go outside, tidying up time. Use of number during routine activities might include, for example, working out how many plates are needed for snack time, counting the number of children present at registration, or counting the number of steps up to the garden area when going outdoors.

1.1 Score yes if there is evidence that children have access to appropriate counting experiences in any form (i.e., during number activities or routines) less than once per week.

1.2 Score yes if there are fewer than three resources (or sets of resources) available. Resources do not need to be accessible daily to give credit. Sets must contain enough objects to be useable as part of a counting activity.

3.1 A few means once a week or more (daily maths activities are not required at this level). See definition above for examples of number activities.

3.2 At least one example must be observed.

3.3 At least two examples should be accessible on a daily basis to give credit.

5.1 Often means daily. Number activities must be seen during the observation to give credit for this indicator. Give credit if at least two examples of spontaneous counting activities with groups or individual children are observed (see All About the ECERS-E for further detail). Alternatively, give credit if there is evidence of a daily maths activity which includes all children, even if you notice adults missing other incidental opportunities for maths learning during the observation. The observer does not need to see examples from all categories (i.e. songs, rhymes, counting books and games) during the observation in order to give credit. However, confirmatory evidence should be sought in the planning, records and display to ensure that all these options are offered at some time.

5.2 At least two examples should be observed. These could take place during group time or free play. Adults must be observed encouraging the children to count.

5.3 At least one example should be observed. Look for evidence of ordinal numbers being used during everyday activities (e.g. talking about who will be first/second/third during a turn-taking game; counting through the days of the month at registration time).

7.1 To give credit at this level, staff should be looking beyond the obvious situations which lend themselves to counting, and bringing number into a wide range of contexts (both formal and informal), with small groups and individuals as well as with the whole group. Several instances should be observed in different contexts.

7.2 To give credit, at least three different examples of activities which explicitly encourage one to one correspondence must be found in the sample of planning reviewed, at least one of which must relate to outdoor activities/play.

7.3 To give credit, specific number activities should be explicitly planned for several times per week.

7.4 Number games, countable objects and books should be accessible to children on a daily basis.

Item	Inadequate		Minimal		Good		Excellent
	1	2	3	4	5	6	7

Item 8. Reading and representing simple numbers

1.1 Attention is not paid to the reading and/ or representation of simple numbers. * P, D, R

1.2 No written numbers are displayed. * D

3.1 Numbers and the equivalent objects are shown next to each other (*e.g. a number frieze showing the number 1 next to one apple, the number 2 next to two pears etc*) D

3.2 Some children occasionally read and/or represent numbers. * P, D, R

3.3 Children's attention is drawn to written number sequence (*e.g. by a number line or by talking to the children about a counting book*)*

5.1 Children are regularly encouraged to read and/or represent simple numbers. * (D) (P) (R)

5.2 Children have materials available which support them in representing numbers (*e.g. number shapes.*) *

7.1 There are planned classroom activities containing numbers and adults encourage children to recognise and represent numbers in a variety of media.* (D) (P) (R)

7.2 Written number work is linked to a practical purpose (*e.g. putting the age on a birthday card*). * D, P, R

Notes for clarification

Children's use of written number at this age should be 'emergent number', i.e. young children's own attempts at representing and recording numbers in a written form. In its earliest stages it may appear as lines and squiggles, or simple 'tallying'. For older children, it might involve writing a shopping list in the home corner and listing how many of each item are needed. Formal writing of numbers is not suggested for children in the ECERS-E age range. Written number work should be linked to a practical purpose and to concrete experiences (e.g. pricing items in a role play shop) rather than through formal activities and/or worksheets.

1.1 Score yes if there is no evidence during the observation, or in planning/records/display that adults draw children's attention to written numbers, or that opportunities are provided for children to recognise and/or represent numbers.

1.2 Numbers should be easily visible to children, i.e. at eye level or large enough to read from a distance.

3.2 Evidence is not required for all children in the group. To give credit, observers should find at least one example of a child (or children) reading number and/or one example of a child (or children) representing number – either during the observation or in the sample of materials (planning, records and display) reviewed.

3.3 At least one example must be observed. Adults should be observed drawing explicit attention to written numbers in sequence, and the numbers should also be spoken aloud so that children associate spoken numbers with the written concepts. This could take place at whole group time, or informally with small groups or individual children.

5.1 Opportunities must be available within the environment which allow and encourage children to recognise and to represent numbers (where appropriate). Observers should look for supporting evidence in the environment, display, planning or records that these opportunities are available regularly (if not daily, then at least 3 times per week). In addition, at least one example of adults explicitly encouraging recognition or representation of number must be observed. This may take place during whole group time or during child-initiated play.

5.2 These do not need to be accessible daily

7.1 Number activities must be planned at least weekly in order to give credit. In addition, observers should see at least two examples of children being encouraged to recognise or write/represent simple numbers in different contexts/media (e.g. drawing numbers in sand/cornflour/paint, reading or writing numbers on the computer, reading numbers in the environment).

7.2 This indicator requires that children are encouraged to use numbers for a practical purpose in order to support their activities within the setting. If this is not observed on the day, at least two examples must be found in the materials reviewed.

Item	Inadequate		Minimal		Good		Excellent
	1	2	3	4	5	6	7

Select either Item 9a or 9b for evidence: choose the one which is most apparent during the observation.

Item 9a. Mathematical activities: Shape

1.1 Little evidence that children have opportunities to experience or learn about shape (*e.g. shape is rarely commented on during ordinary play or daily routines, adults do not plan activities which involve shapes*). * P, D, R	3.1 Some different shapes are accessible to children. *	5.1 A wide variety of shapes are accessible and adults draw children's attention to shape names, (*e.g. circle, square, triangle, rectangle*). *	7.1 Many activities and materials are available which encourage children to generalise shape across a variety of contexts, (*e.g. art activities, construction activities, group play arrangements, role-play*). * (P) (R) (D)
	3.2 Shapes are named outside planned shape activities. *	5.2 Staff draw children's attention to shape in their own work (*e.g. drawings, models*). *	7.2 Activities develop and extend concepts beyond basic shapes (*e.g. to include properties of two or three dimensional shapes*). P, R, D
	3.3 Shape is an explicit part of some activities. * P, D, R		7.3 Staff encourage children to understand the properties of different shapes (*e.g. 3 sides of a triangle*) and to use this understanding to solve shape puzzles and apply their knowledge to new situations. * D, P, R

Notes for clarification

1.1 Score yes if no references to shape are seen during the observation and there is no evidence in planning, records or display that work on shape has been carried out in the past.

3.1 Any resources with different shaped pieces can be counted e.g. blocks with different shaped pieces, shape cutters for cooking/play dough activities, shapes displayed on the wall. At least two examples should be accessible on a daily basis to give credit.

3.2 Staff members are not required to use the proper names for shapes, to give credit for this indicator: common names are acceptable e.g. tube. Other pattern-related language is also acceptable as evidence e.g. pointy, wavy. At least one example of staff using shape or pattern language should be observed to give credit.

3.3 Give credit if an explicit shape activity is observed. If planning, records or display are used as evidence, at least two different examples must be found in the sample of materials reviewed.

5.1 A good selection of shape resources (5 or more examples) should be accessible on a every day basis to give credit (e.g. a shape poster, a set of shape puzzles, a set of 3D shapes, a set of blocks of different shapes and a book on shapes in the book area). Others may be available but not accessible daily. A wider variety of different shapes should also be accessible than is expected in indicator 3.1. In addition to the availability of resources, observers should hear at least two examples of adults drawing attention to shape names.

5.2 At least one example must be observed.

7.1 At least three examples must be evident on the day of the observation, although confirmatory evidence can be found in the sample of materials reviewed.

7.3 The emphasis here is on applying knowledge of shape.

Item	Inadequate 1	2	Minimal 3	4	Good 5	6	Excellent 7

Item 9b. Mathematical activities: Sorting, matching and comparing

1.1 Children are not encouraged to sort, match or compare objects and materials. * P, D, R

3.1 Some items to support sorting, comparing and/or matching are accessible. *

3.2 Children sort, compare and/or match by at least one identifiable criterion (*e.g. heavy/light or by colour*). * P, D, R

3.3 Staff demonstrate sorting, comparing or matching and allow the children to participate. *

5.1 Activities occur regularly which develop and extend sorting, comparing and matching skills (*e.g. sorting by more than one criterion, sorting in different contexts or using objects in the child's everyday environment*). * (P)

5.2 Characteristics which form the basis for sorting, matching and comparing are made explicit by the adults.

5.3 Staff encourage children to use comparative language when sorting, matching, comparing or measuring (*e.g. big, bigger, biggest, bigger/ smaller*).*

7.1 Children are encouraged to identify the characteristics of sets of objects which form the basis for sorting, matching or comparing (*e.g. to explain why a set of shapes is alike by saying 'They are all circles'*). *

7.2 Language which explores sorting, comparing or matching is used in a variety of contexts across a range of activities (*e.g. ordering the size of the three bears; using words such as curlier, bigger, heavier.*).*

7.3 Children are encouraged to complete a sorting/ matching/ comparing activity, then repeat using a different criterion (*including their own*) *as the basis for sorting/ matching/ comparing (e.g. arrange hats by size then by shape.*) * P

Notes for clarification

1.1 Score yes if no references to sorting, matching or comparing are seen during the observation and there is no evidence in planning, records or display that such work has been carried out in the past.

3.1 Examples of items which could be matched, sorted or compared include everyday objects such as collections of natural materials (pebbles, pine cones, shells) and different shaped or sized resources (e.g. containers for sand/water play, blocks) as well as the more commercial 'counting' resources such as counting bears, unifix cubes or sorting/matching games. At least two examples should be accessible on a daily basis to give credit.

3.2 Give credit if children are observed sorting, matching or comparing (with or without adults) during the observation. If planning, records or display are used as evidence, at least two different examples must be found in the sample of materials reviewed.

3.3 At least one example should be observed, and must involve staff actively demonstrating or supporting sorting/matching/comparing. This might take place as part of a planned adult-led activity, or more informally with a small number of children (e.g. showing children how to sort resources when tidying away, pointing out the fact that two children have matching coloured tops and encouraging them to identify others wearing the same colour, encouraging a child to make a tower using, say, only red bricks).

5.1 At least one example should be observed. Observers should also check planning for regularity (regularly means at least 3 to 4 times per week).

5.3 At least one example must be observed. The focus here is on staff encouraging children to use comparative language.

7.1 At least one example must be observed.

7.2 At least two different examples must be observed.

7.3 If this is not observed on the day, at least one explicit example must be seen in the sample of materials reviewed.

Item	Inadequate		Minimal		Good		Excellent
	1	2	3	4	5	6	7

Science and Environment N.B. Items 10 and 11 MUST be assessed. After assessing Items 10 and 11 you may then select EITHER Item 12a, Item 12b or Item 12c for evidence. Choose the item that is most apparent during the observation. This science subscale may require access to planning documents.

Item 10. Natural materials *

1.1 There is little access indoors to natural materials (fewer than 3 examples).	3.1 Some natural materials are accessible to the children indoors.*	5.1 Natural materials are used beyond decoration to illustrate specific concepts, (*e.g. planting seeds or bulbs to illustrate growth, seed dispersal*). P, D *	7.1 Children are encouraged to identify and explore a range of natural phenomena in their environment outside the centre and talk about/describe them. (P, D) *
	3.2 Natural materials are accessible outdoors.*	5.2 Children are often encouraged to explore the characteristics of natural materials. *	7.2 Children are encouraged to bring natural materials into the centre. D, Q*
		5.3 Adults show appreciation, curiosity and/or respect for nature when with children (*e.g. interest in, rather than fear or disgust of, fungi or worms*). *	7.3 Children are encouraged to make close observations of natural objects and/or draw them. P, D, R *

Notes for clarification

Natural materials include living things (e.g. plants, fish, hamsters, etc), collections of natural objects (e.g., pebbles, pine cones, shells, etc) and other natural materials such as sand and water. Materials should be in their natural state and recognisable as coming from the natural environment.

3.1 At least 5 different examples should be accessible daily. Others may be available but not accessible every day (e.g. those which cannot be left out for safety reasons).

3.2 At least 5 different examples should be accessible daily. Examples might include: trees which are accessible to children; gardens/planting areas e.g. herbs, vegetable plots; animals kept outdoors e.g. rabbit, guinea pig.

5.1 Give credit if this is observed on the day. If evidence is taken solely from planning/display, at least two different examples should be evident in the materials reviewed. At this level, the planning should include an explicit reference to the idea/scientific concept being introduced (e.g. 'observing and drawing butterflies over time to understand their life cycle' rather than 'drawing butterflies').

5.2 Often means every day. Give credit if one or more examples are observed. This could include informal discussion (e.g. feeling the texture of a pebble found in the playground; looking at mini-beasts under stones) as well as planned activities (e.g. cutting up fruits to look at the pips).

5.3 At least one example must be observed.

7.1 At least one discussion relating to natural phenomena/materials should be observed and children should be seen to take an active role in the discussion. Planning or display evidence can be used as supporting evidence that children are encouraged to explore a range of natural phenomena (e.g. weather, mini-beasts, plants, animals, Forest School). Planning should also provide some evidence of planning for talk e.g. key vocabulary.

7.2 Give credit if an example is observed on the day (e.g., staff set up a nature trail in the garden and encourage children to find objects for discussion at group time). Credit can also be given for recent display evidence showing children bringing natural materials into the centre (e.g. a pet from home; gathering leaves in Autumn). If not observed or seen in display, an open-ended question can be asked, for example: 'How do you collect the natural materials for your topics and/or displays?'; 'Could you give me some examples of when children have brought in natural materials they were interested in?'. Do not give credit unless specific examples can be provided.

7.3 Give credit if this is observed. If planning, records or display are used, at least one example should be evident in the sample of materials reviewed (and this should be explicit enough to suggest that children have been encouraged to observe natural materials closely).

Item	Inadequate 1	2	Minimal 3	4	Good 5	6	Excellent 7

Item 11. Areas featuring science/science resources

Inadequate	Minimal	Good	Excellent
1.1 No evidence of science resources, displays, books or activities.	3.1 Science provision includes a selection of items (*e.g. magnets or hand lenses*). *	5.1 A variety of science equipment is accessible for children to use. *	7.1 A wide range of science equipment is available. *
	3.2 Displays show evidence of natural change (*e.g. seasons*). * D	5.2 There is evidence of collections of things with similar and/or different properties, (*e.g. things that roll, stretch, bounce, are made of plastic, of metal*). *	7.2 A range of reference materials is available including books, pictures, reference charts and photographs. * D
	3.3 Display/s which could be used to generate discussion about science in the world around us are visible to the children (*e.g. posters of the body, life cycle of a butterfly*). * D	5.3 Print resources go beyond story books to some reference books or material on science topics. *	7.3 A large and stimulating science area is set up for the children to use daily.
			7.4 Science materials feature in other areas of the centre as well as the one set aside for science. *

Notes for clarification

3.1 At least two examples should be accessible on a daily basis.

3.2 The intention of this indicator is that adults have made an effort to 'bring the outdoors in' and/or provide an opportunity for children to consider changes in the natural world.

3.3 The display must have a science purpose (e.g. posters showing pets or a generic woodland scene would not be adequate).

5.1 Variety means more of each type of item (so that several children can use the materials at once) but also a greater variety of items than is required for 3.1. At least five different examples should be accessible daily to give credit. Only give credit for general sand and water materials (e.g. funnels/ containers/ plastic tubes) if there is evidence that these are used for the learning of science, for example exploring sinking and floating.

5.2 There must be evidence that collections have been put together on the basis of their scientific properties and not, for example, because they are all the same colour. Collections do not need to be accessible every day.

5.3 At least 5 examples (e.g. 5 science books) should be accessible daily to give credit.

7.1 As required for 5.1 plus examples of more specialised science materials which relate to specific topics e.g. colour (coloured lenses, colour paddles), light (prisms, light boxes), electricity (batteries, wires). These more specialised items do not need to be accessible to the children on a daily basis.

7.2 Examples of all four categories should be available within the setting and easily accessible to adults so they can refer to them when needed. A smaller range (representing several of the categories) should be accessible to the children daily. Pictures might include posters or other display.

7.4 For example, a seaside role play area supplemented with reference books on seaside creatures, a crab claw and a hand lens so the children can make close observations.

Item	Inadequate		Minimal		Good		Excellent
	1	2	3	4	5	6	7

Select one of Items 12a, 12b or 12c for evidence: choose the one for which you can find the most detailed evidence.

In order to assess the higher levels you must have observed staff interacting with children e.g. at the water/sand trough or other activity area. At these levels, evidence is being sought for engagement with children in scientific processes i.e. close observation, raising questions/making guesses (hypothesising), experimenting (see what happens) and communicating and interpreting results (why has this happened).

Item 12a. Science activities: Non-living

1.1 Children are not encouraged to explore aspects of their physicalenvironment. Scientific words and concepts do not feature in discussions. * P, D, R,

3.1 Some science exploration or experiments are carried out by adults or children (*e.g. ice cubes put out in sun*). * P, D, R,

3.2 Scientific words and/or concepts are mentioned daily.
(*e.g. discussing the weather; using the words floating and sinking at the water tray; talking about melting, pressure, why/how things move*). *

5.1 Staff often plan and introduce appropriate scientific concepts (*e.g. how materials change, magnetism, sinkers and floaters*) and children handle materials. * P, D, R

5.2 Adults draw attention to characteristics or changes in materials (*e.g. birthday candles melting*). *

5.3 Children are encouraged to use more than one sense to explore non-living phenomena and talk about their experience (*e.g. touch/smell as well as sight*). *

7.1 Children have hands on experience in varied science activities exploring non-living materials.* (P, D, R)

7.2 Children are encouraged to experience a range of scientific concepts/ideas.* P, D, R

7.3 Adults engage children in discussion about materials and their characteristics. *

7.4 Adults encourage children to ask questions. *

7.5 Adults support children in systematically seeking answers to questions. *

7.6 Children are encouraged to record results of scientific enquiry.

40

Notes for clarification

1.1 Score yes if no examples are observed and no evidence is found in the planning/ records/ display reviewed.

3.1 Give credit if this is observed. If planning, records or display are used as evidence, at least two different examples must be found in the sample of materials reviewed. Examples might include investigating the friction of different surfaces for toy cars, or the insulation/ absorbency properties of different materials (e.g. which material will keep our doll the warmest/ driest?).

3.2 At least one example must be observed, and must relate to non-living processes. This could take place during a planned science activity, or during everyday/ informal activities or play.

5.1 This indicator requires that staff plan for science learning. At least four different examples relating to non-living processes must be found in the sample of materials (planning, records and display) reviewed. At this level, the planning should include an explicit reference to the idea/scientific concept being introduced (e.g. 'investigating which materials are magnetic and non-magnetic' rather than 'magnet play'). The second part of the indicator requires that children have the opportunity to handle materials (i.e. that staff do not simply demonstrate experiments for children to watch).

5.2 To give credit adults must be observed drawing attention either to characteristics or to change at least once (e.g. drawing attention to water evaporating from the ground on a hot day). At this level, the talk should be more scientific than is required for 3.2.

5.3 At least one example must be observed to give credit. As well as being encouraged to use more than once sense, children should also be encouraged to talk about their experience using descriptive language (e.g. 'What does it smell like?').

7.1 In order to assess whether activities are introduced in a hands-on way, at least one science activity must have been observed (e.g. exploring magnets and magnetic objects) – although not all children need to have taken part on that day. Evidence from planning, records and display should also be reviewed to assess the variety in 'non-living' activities provided (and this evidence should also point to a hands-on approach for all children).

7.2 In order to give credit, a broader range of concepts and ideas should be evident in the materials reviewed than is required for indicator 5.1.

7.3, 7.4, 7.5 At least one example must be observed but one or more high quality interactions may provide examples of 7.3, 7.4, 7.5.

Item	Inadequate		Minimal		Good		Excellent
	1	2	3	4	5	6	7

Item 12b. Science activities: Living processes and the world around us

In order to assess the higher levels you must have observed staff interacting with children e.g. in the outdoor area. At these levels, evidence is being sought for engagement with children in scientific processes i.e. close observation, raising questions/making guesses (hypothesising), experimenting (seeing what happens) and communicating and interpreting results (why has this happened?).

1.1 Children are not encouraged to explore aspects of their natural environment and scientific words and concepts do not feature in discussions. * P, D, R

3.1 Some science exploration or experiments are carried out by adults or children (*e.g. growing seedlings, keeping tadpoles*). * P, D, R

3.2 Scientific words and concepts are mentioned daily (*e.g. plant growth, insect habitats, the cycle of life, caring for living things*). *

3.3 Living things are present, either indoors or outdoors (*e.g. plants, fish, snails*).

5.1 Staff often plan and introduce appropriate scientific concepts and children handle materials. * P, D, R

5.2 Adults draw attention to characteristics or changes in the natural world (*e.g. the life cycle of a butterfly, the ageing process, the different parts of a flower*). *

5.3 Children are encouraged to use more than one sense to explore living phenomena and talk about their experience (*e.g. touch/smell as well as sight*) *

7.1 All children have hands-on experience with living things where appropriate. * (P, D, R)

7.2 Children are encouraged to experience a range of scientific concepts/ideas.* P, D, R

7.3 Adults engage the children in discussion about both plant and animal worlds and their characteristics. *

7.4 Adults encourage children to ask questions. *

7.5 Adults support children in systematically seeking answers to questions. *

7.6 Children are encouraged to record results of scientific enquiry.

Notes for clarification

1.1 Score yes if no examples are observed and no evidence is found in the planning, records or display reviewed.

3.1 Give credit if this is observed. If planning, records or display are used as evidence, at least two different examples relating to living processes must be found in the sample of materials reviewed.

3.2 At least one example must be observed, and must relate to living processes. This could take place during a planned science activity, or during everyday/ informal activities or play. Examples might include discussing pets owned by the children or looking at a spider found in the playground.

5.1 This indicator requires that staff plan for science learning. At least four different examples relating to living processes must be found in the sample of materials (planning, records and display) reviewed. At this level, the planning should include an explicit reference to the idea/scientific concept being introduced (e.g. 'observing and drawing butterflies over time to understand their life cycle' rather than 'drawing butterflies'). The second part of the indicator requires that children have the opportunity to handle materials (i.e. that staff do not simply demonstrate experiments for children to watch).

5.2 To give credit, adults must be observed drawing attention either to characteristics or to change at least once. At this level, the talk should be more scientific than is required for 3.2.

5.3 To give credit, at least one example must be observed. As well as being encouraged to use more than one sense, children should be encouraged to talk about their experience using descriptive language (e.g. 'What does it feel like?').

7.1 In order to assess whether activities are introduced in a hands-on way, at least one science activity must have been observed (e.g., planting seeds, hunting for and collecting mini-beasts) – although not all children need to be observed taking part. Evidence from planning, records and display should also be reviewed to assess the variety in 'living-processes' activities provided (and this evidence should also point to a hands-on approach for all children).

7.2 In order to give credit, a broader range of concepts and ideas should be evident in the materials reviewed than is required for indicator 5.1.

7.3 At least one example of discussion relating to the plant world and one to the animal world must be observed, to give credit.

7.3, 7.4, 7.5 At least one example must be observed but one or more high quality interaction may provide examples of 7.3, 7.4, 7.5.

Item	Inadequate		Minimal		Good		Excellent
	1	2	3	4	5	6	7

Item 12c. Science activities: Food preparation `

In order to assess the higher levels you must have observed staff interacting with children e.g. at snack time or during a cooking activity. At these levels, evidence is being sought for engagement with children in scientific processes i.e. close observation, raising questions/making guesses (hypothesising), experimenting (seeing what happens) and communicating and interpreting results (why has this happened?).

1.1 No preparation of food or drink is undertaken with the children. * P, D, R, Q	3.1 Food preparation is sometimes undertaken with the children. * P, D, R, Q	5.1 Food preparation/cooking activities are often provided. * P, D, R, Q	7.1 A variety of cooking activities (in which all children have the opportunity to take part) is often provided. P
	3.2 Some children have the opportunity to participate in food preparation. * P, D, Q	5.2 Most of the children have the opportunity to participate in food preparation. * P, D, R, Q	7.2 The end result is attractive, edible and valued (*e.g. eaten by children, taken home*).
	3.3 Some food-related discussion takes place where appropriate (*e.g. staff and children talk about food at snack time or during a cooking activity*). *	5.3 The staff lead discussion about the food involved and use appropriate language (*e.g. melt, dissolve*). *	7.3 The staff lead and encourage discussion on the process of food preparation and/or question children about it (*e.g. what did it look like before, what does it look like now, what has happened to it?*). *
		5.4 Children are encouraged to use more than one sense (*e.g. feel, smell, taste*) to explore individual ingredients and talk about their experiences. *	

Notes for clarification

Food preparation includes cooking activities and also the preparation of food for snack or meal times (which children may observe or participate in).

1.1 Score yes if children do not have the opportunity to observe (or participate) in food preparation/cooking during the observation, there is no evidence in the planning, records and display reviewed that children are ever offered this experience, or staff (when asked) cannot provide examples of such activities taking place.

3.1 This might include children observing a member of staff preparing food. If planning, records or display are used as evidence, at least two examples must be found in the sample of materials reviewed.

3.2 This may be spontaneous (e.g. some children helping to prepare food for snack or lunch time) or planned in advance (e.g. planned cooking activities). If planning, records or display are used as evidence, at least two examples must be found in the sample of materials reviewed.

3.3 At least one example must be observed. Examples at snack or meal time might include a discussion about burnt toast, new biscuits or food brought in by the children.

5.1/5.2 Often means approximately every 1 to 2 weeks or more frequently. Credit can be given at 5.1 if food preparation activities are offered every 1 to 2 weeks (even if not all children have a chance to participate this frequently). To give credit at 5.2, the majority of children should have an opportunity to take part in food preparation at least once every 1 to 2 weeks.

5.3 This must be observed at least once. At this level, the talk should be more scientific than is required for 3.3.

5.4 At least one example must be observed. As well as being encouraged to use more than one sense, children should also be encouraged to talk about their experience using descriptive language (e.g. 'What does it smell like?).

7.3 This must be observed at least once. Children must be actively involved in the discussion, and staff should be observed supporting and scaffolding the children's scientific language and learning.

Item	Inadequate		Minimal		Good		Excellent
	1	2	3	4	5	6	7

Diversity

Item 13. Planning for individual learning needs
Ask to see the records kept on individual children

1.1 Activities and resources are not matched to different ages, developmental stages or interests. P, Q *	3.1 Some additional provision is made in terms of developmental stage, or for individuals or groups with specific needs such as learning support or English language support. P, Q *	5.1 The range of activities provided draws on children's interests and caters for all developmental stages and backgrounds, enabling all children in the group to participate in a satisfying and cognitively demanding way. * P Q	7.1 The organisation of social interaction enables children of all developmental stages and backgrounds to participate at an appropriate level in both individual and common tasks (*e.g. pairing children of different ages and abilities for certain tasks*). * Q
1.2 Planning is not written down. P *	3.2 Some of the written planning shows differentiation for particular individuals or groups. P *	5.2 Day to day plans are drawn up with the specific aim of developing activities that will satisfy the interests and needs of each child, either individually or as groups. * P	7.2 Planning sheets identify the role of the adult when working with individuals/pairs/groups of children. Planning also shows a range of capability levels at which a task or activity may be experienced. * P
1.3 Written planning takes no account of specific individuals or groups. P *	3.3 Written records indicate some awareness of how individuals have coped with activities, or of the appropriateness of activities (*e.g. needs bilingual support, able to count to 2*). * R	5.3 Children are observed frequently and individual records are kept on their progress in different aspects of their development. * R	7.3 Observations and records of progress are used to inform planning. * P, R, Q
1.4 No records are kept, or the records kept describe activities rather than the child's response or success in that activity, (*e.g. ticked checklists or samples of children's work*) R	3.4 Staff show some awareness of the need to support and recognise children's differences, publicly praising children of all abilities. *	5.4 Staff consistently draw children's attention to difference in a positive way. * (D)	7.4 Staff specifically plan activities which draw the attention of the whole group to difference and capability in a positive way (*e.g. showing children who are disabled in a positive light, celebrating bilingualism*). * P, D, R

Notes for clarification

Activities and planning

1.1, 3.1, 5.1; 1.2, 3.2, 5.2 There should be evidence that differentiated activities and/or resources are offered to children with particular needs (e.g. who have EAL) and according to age and developmental stage.

- 1.1, 3.1 and 5.1 relate to the provision/adaptation of activities and resources offered to children (whether these are planned or informal) and the extent to which these cater for differing needs.
- 1.2, 3.2 and 5.2 specifically assess the extent to which differentiation is *planned for.*

Examples of appropriate differentiation can be found in 'All About the ECERS-E'.

5.1, 5.2 The range of activities should provide for all children (e.g. children of different ages/stages, children with English as an additional language) and not simply those with identified special needs.

7.1 It may be necessary to ask about this as it will not always be apparent why children have been encouraged to work together on a task. For example: 'Why have you encouraged those children to work together?'; 'Do you ever encourage particular children to work together? Why? Can you give some examples?'

7.2 The adult guidance should be more detailed than simply listing which adult works with which activity/group. Both elements of the indicator (i.e. the adult guidance and the range of capability levels) must be met in order to give credit.

Observations and record-keeping

3.3 At this level credit can be given for records/observations which show fairly minimal awareness of how individuals have coped with activities or of the appropriateness of activities.

5.3 To give credit, children should be observed weekly (or almost weekly) in some way. This may take the form of post-it notes recording specific incidents or achievements rather than formal observations. Records of progress do not need to be updated weekly.

7.3 It may be necessary to ask a question to establish whether this happens (for example, ask staff to provide or show specific examples of observations being used to inform planning).

Celebrating difference

3.4 Give credit if it is clearly part of usual practice to praise all children in the group regularly.

5.4 This indicator relates to celebration of differences among children in the group. To give credit, the discussion must be more specific than is required for 3.4 (e.g. drawing specific attention to a new skill a child has mastered; a sensitive discussion with the group at lunchtime about why a certain child doesn't eat meat; explaining in an appropriate way why a child with a disability needs to sit on a special chair). At least one example must be observed, and supporting evidence may also be found in display (e.g. children's work displayed with specific comments about their achievements).

7.4 This indicator goes beyond the children in the group to consider the celebration of difference more generally. Observers should check planning for evidence that celebration of difference and capability are specifically planned for (e.g. discussing blindness and deafness as part of a topic on senses). Evidence may also be found in displays or children's records. At least one example of explicit planning for celebration of difference should be found in the materials reviewed, to give credit.

Item	Inadequate		Minimal		Good		Excellent
	1	2	3	4	5	6	7

Item 14. Gender equality and awareness

1.1 Where books, pictures, small world figures, dolls and/or displays portray gender, few of them challenge gender stereotypes.* D

1.2 The staff ignore or encourage stereotyped gender behaviours (*e.g. only girls are praised for looking pretty or boys for being strong*).*

3.1 Some books, pictures, small world figures, dolls and/or displays which challenge gender stereotypes are accessible to the children (*e.g. father looking after baby, female soldier, photos of both boys and girls playing with the large blocks*). * D

3.2 Children's activities and behaviour sometimes cross gender stereotypes (*e.g. boys cooking or caring for dolls in the home corner, girls playing outside on large mobile toys*).

5.1 Many books, pictures, small world figures, dolls and/or displays show males and females in non-stereotypical roles (*e.g. male childcare worker, woman changing a tyre*). * D

5.2 Participation in activities which cross gender boundaries is common practice and/ or adults explicitly encourage this where necessary (*e.g. all children are expected – but not forced – to join in construction activities and dance*). * (Q)

5.3 Dressing-up clothes encourage non-stereotyped cross-gender roles (e.g. *unisex nurse or police outfits; non-gendered clothing such as dungarees*). * (P) (Q)

7.1 The children's attention is specifically drawn to books, pictures, small world figures, dolls and/or displays that show males and females in non-stereotypical roles, and/or specific activities are developed to help the children discuss gender. * P, Q

7.2 Staff are confident in discussing and challenging the stereotypical behaviours and assumptions of children. Q

7.3 Male educators are employed to work with children and/or men are sometimes invited to work in the centre with the children. * Q

Notes for clarification

1.1 Only score yes if there is very little or no evidence of resources which counter stereotypes, e.g. less than 1 in 10 (10%) of resources which relate to gender. Credit can be given for resources of one type if these are plentiful enough (e.g. many books but no pictures, small world figures, dolls or displays).

1.2 Only score down if several examples (or one very explicit example) of stereotyping, or of staff ignoring stereotypical behaviour/comments, are seen during the observation.

3.1 Overall, 10% (or more) of the resources which portray gender should be non-stereotypical to give credit. Examples from 2 of the 5 categories should be evident and accessible to children on a daily basis.

5.1 Overall, 20% (or more) of the accessible resources which portray gender should be non-stereotypical to give credit. Examples from 3 of the 5 categories should be evident and accessible on a daily basis (although many examples in every category are not required).

5.2 Observers should look for evidence that all children access activities and areas which might be associated with one gender (e.g. woodworking bench, playing with dolls in the home corner, active gross motor play). If this is seen to be common practice, credit can be given. If however one gender appears to dominate a particular activity and staff do not act to address this (e.g. by encouraging boys to join play in the home corner) then score down. It may be necessary to ask a question to discover any particular strategies employed (e.g. if certain times are set aside for girls to play on very active gross motor equipment). However, unless a specific answer is given to any question asked, this indicator should be scored based on observed behaviour of children and staff.

5.3 If appropriate dressing-up resources are seen to be available but stored so they are not accessible to children each day, the observer should check planning or ask a question to discover how often they are made accessible. Give credit if dressing-up clothes which encourage non-gender roles are accessible to children twice a week or more.

7.1 Give credit if one or more examples are observed. Observable examples might include staff reading and discussing stories like *The Paperbag Princess* or *Mrs Plug the Plumber* which challenge traditional role-models. If non-stereotypical books and resources are present but adults are not observed using them, ask a non-leading question such as 'Did you choose these resources for a particular reason?' or 'Could you give me an example of how you use these books/resources?' Credit can also be given if explicit evidence is found in the planning of activities to help children discuss gender (at least one example in the sample of planning reviewed).

7.2 If this is not observed, the indicator may be scored using a question (e.g. 'What would you do if a child suggested girls were not allowed to play with the tools because 'fixing things is a man's job?). Alternatively, the observer might ask for examples of occasions when children have said something sexist and how this was dealt with. Unless a very specific answer is given to any question asked, this indicator should be scored based on what is observed.

7.3 If male educators are not employed to work with the children, credit can be given if men are invited in to the centre to take part in activities with the children at least 3 times a year.

Item	Inadequate		Minimal		Good		Excellent
	1	2	3	4	5	6	7

Item 15. Race equality and awareness

1.1 Books, pictures, small world figures, dolls and displays show little evidence of ethnic diversity in our society or the wider world. * D

3.1 The children sometimes play with toys, resources or materials from cultures other than the ethnic majority. * P, D, R

5.1 Children play with toys, resources or materials drawn from a range of cultures (*e.g. range of appropriate and non-stereotypical dressing-up clothes, cooking and eating utensils used in dramatic play, musical instruments*). * (P)

7.1 Staff develop activities with the express purpose of promoting cultural understanding (*e.g. attention is drawn to similarities and differences in things and people, different cultures are routinely brought into topic work, visitors and performers reflect a range of cultures*). * P, D, R, Q

1.2 Negative, stereotyped or offensive images are on view to the children (*e.g. a golliwog, Red Indians*). D

3.2 Books, pictures, small world figures, dolls and/or displays show people from a variety of ethnic groups. * D

5.2 Some books, pictures, small world figures, dolls and/or displays show people from different ethnic groups in non-stereotypical roles (*e.g. as scientists, doctors, engineers, office workers in suits*). * D

7.2 Specific activities are developed to promote understanding of difference (*e.g. paints are mixed to match skin tones to visibly show subtlety in differences*). * P, D, R, Q

5.3 Some images or activities show children that they have much in common with people from other cultural groups (*e.g. images which stress physical similarities or similarities in rituals and day-to-day activities*). * P, D

7.3 Minority ethnic educators are employed in the centre, and/or black and minority ethnic people are sometimes invited into the setting to work with the children. Q

5.4 Staff intervene appropriately when a child or an adult in the setting shows prejudice. * Q

Notes for clarification

1.1/3.1/5.1 Resources should be clearly visible and in areas frequently used by the children.

3.1 The resources may not be out every day but there should be evidence that stored/ borrowed toys or resources (e.g. cooking utensils/foods, dressing up clothes, real or imitation musical instruments) from other cultures are sometimes used, for example boxes of resources available for celebration of different festivals during the year, or resources representing different cultures accessible in the home corner. Resources representing at least 2 cultures other than the majority culture should be available at some time (not necessarily daily). If no toys or resources are accessible on the day of the visit, observers should look at stored resources, and also for evidence in planning, display and/or records, that such materials are available and used.

3.2 A variety of different ethnic, cultural and/or religious groups should be represented (e.g. at least 3) and examples should be found in 2 of the 5 categories listed (i.e. books, pictures, small world figures, dolls and displays). If the group is diverse, photographs of the children themselves can be counted. At this level, credit can also be given for images which are tokenistic or stereotypical, e.g. other nationalities portrayed only in national dress; Africans shown only in traditional rural setting; black dolls with white features; books such as *Handa's Surprise* in the book selection but no stories or pictures of African children living in a western culture. Do not give credit for images which are offensive.

5.1 To give credit for this indicator, there should be evidence of more than occasional tokenistic celebration of other cultures/festivals (which can be credited in indicator 3.1). Race equality and multicultural awareness should be embedded in the ethos of the setting. Resources from 2 or more cultures should be accessible daily, and resources from at least 2 other available at some time (not necessarily daily). Planning can provide supporting evidence of the range of cultures included in day-to-day activities and celebrations.

5.2 At least 3 different examples should be visible/accessible daily (across at least 2 of the 5 categories).

5.3 Similarities and differences must be explicitly shown in display and/or planning. Children should receive a constant message that all children do similar everyday things (e.g. go to the park, attend weddings). Two or more examples are required in the display or planning reviewed.

5.4 If no prejudice is shown, use a question such as 'what would you do if one of the children showed prejudice towards another, or made a racist remark?' Give credit for this indicator if the answer indicates a sensitive approach: the child should not be blamed, but told that their words and/or behaviour are inappropriate/ inaccurate. The adult should then provide a correct explanation and suggest a more appropriate response.

7.1, 7.2 These indicators assess the extent to which staff use activities so as to take children beyond simple recognition and into understanding and respect of different races and cultures. For each indicator at least three explicit examples must be found in the materials reviewed (or given as answers to questions).

ECERS-E Score sheet

Centre/School	Centre code/URN	Date	Observer
Time observation began	Time observation ended		

LITERACY SUBSCALE

1. Print in the environment   1   2   3   4   5   6   7

Y N	Y N	Y N	Y N
1.1 ☐ ☐ D	3.1 ☐ ☐ D	5.1 ☐ ☐ D	7.1 ☐ ☐
1.2 ☐ ☐ D	3.2 ☐ ☐	5.2 ☐ ☐	7.2 ☐ ☐
	3.3 ☐ ☐ D	5.3 ☐ ☐	7.3 ☐ ☐

4. Sounds in words   1   2   3   4   5   6   7

Y N	Y N	Y N	Y N
1.1 ☐ ☐ PQ	3.1 ☐ ☐ PQ	5.1 ☐ ☐	7.1 ☐ ☐ P
	3.2 ☐ ☐	5.2 ☐ ☐	7.2 ☐ ☐ (P)

2. Book and literacy areas   1   2   3   4   5   6   7

Y N	Y N	Y N	Y N
1.1 ☐ ☐	3.1 ☐ ☐	5.1 ☐ ☐	7.1 ☐ ☐
1.2 ☐ ☐	3.2 ☐ ☐	5.2 ☐ ☐	7.2 ☐ ☐
	3.3 ☐ ☐		7.3 ☐ ☐

5. Emergent writing/mark making   1   2   3   4   5   6   7

Y N	Y N	Y N	Y N
1.1 ☐ ☐	3.1 ☐ ☐	5.1 ☐ ☐	7.1 ☐ ☐
1.2 ☐ ☐ DR	3.2 ☐ ☐	5.2 ☐ ☐	7.2 ☐ ☐ (P) D R
	3.3 ☐ ☐ DR	5.3 ☐ ☐	7.3 ☐ ☐ D

3. Adult reading with the children   1   2   3   4   5   6   7

Y N	Y N	Y N	Y N
1.1 ☐ ☐ PQ	3.1 ☐ ☐ PQ	5.1 ☐ ☐	7.1 ☐ ☐
	3.2 ☐ ☐	5.2 ☐ ☐	7.2 ☐ ☐ D
			7.3 ☐ ☐

6. Talking and listening   1   2   3   4   5   6   7

Y N	Y N	Y N	Y N
1.1 ☐ ☐	3.1 ☐ ☐	5.1 ☐ ☐ (P)	7.1 ☐ ☐
1.2 ☐ ☐	3.2 ☐ ☐	5.2 ☐ ☐	7.2 ☐ ☐ P
		5.3 ☐ ☐	7.3 ☐ ☐
			7.4 ☐ ☐

MATHEMATICAL SUBSCALE

7. Counting and the application of counting   1 2 3 4 5 6 7

	Y N		Y N		Y N		Y N
1.1	☐ ☐ PDRQ	3.1	☐ ☐ PDRQ	5.1	☐ ☐ (P D R)	7.1	☐ ☐
1.2	☐ ☐	3.2	☐ ☐	5.2	☐ ☐	7.2	☐ ☐ P
		3.3	☐ ☐ D	5.3	☐ ☐	7.3	☐ ☐ P
						7.4	☐ ☐

9a. Shape   1 2 3 4 5 6 7 NA

	Y N		Y N		Y N		Y N
1.1	☐ ☐ PDR	3.1	☐ ☐	5.1	☐ ☐	7.1	☐ ☐ (P D R)
		3.2	☐ ☐	5.2	☐ ☐	7.2	☐ ☐ P D R
		3.3	☐ ☐ PDR			7.3	☐ ☐ P D R

8. Reading and representing simple numbers   1 2 3 4 5 6 7

	Y N		Y N		Y N		Y N
1.1	☐ ☐ PDR	3.1	☐ ☐ D	5.1	☐ ☐ (P D R)	7.1	☐ ☐ (P D R)
1.2	☐ ☐ D	3.2	☐ ☐ PDR	5.2	☐ ☐	7.2	☐ ☐ P D R
		3.3	☐ ☐				

9b. Sorting, matching and comparing   1 2 3 4 5 6 7 NA

	Y N		Y N		Y N		Y N
1.1	☐ ☐ PDR	3.1	☐ ☐	5.1	☐ ☐ (P)	7.1	☐ ☐
		3.2	☐ ☐ PDR	5.2	☐ ☐	7.2	☐ ☐
		3.3	☐ ☐	5.3	☐ ☐	7.3	☐ ☐ P

SCIENCE AND ENVIRONMENT SUBSCALE

10. Natural materials   1   2   3   4   5   6   7

Y N	Y N	Y N	Y N
1.1 ☐ ☐	3.1 ☐ ☐	5.1 ☐ ☐ P D	7.1 ☐ ☐ (P D)
	3.2 ☐ ☐	5.2 ☐ ☐	7.2 ☐ ☐ D Q
		5.3 ☐ ☐	7.3 ☐ ☐ P D R

11. Areas featuring science/science resources   1   2   3   4   5   6   7

Y N	Y N	Y N	Y N
1.1 ☐ ☐	3.1 ☐ ☐	5.1 ☐ ☐	7.1 ☐ ☐
	3.2 ☐ ☐ D	5.2 ☐ ☐	7.2 ☐ ☐ D
	3.3 ☐ ☐ D	5.3 ☐ ☐	7.3 ☐ ☐
			7.4 ☐ ☐

12a. Science activities: Non Living   1   2   3   4   5   6   7   NA

Y N	Y N	Y N	Y N
1.1 ☐ ☐ PDR	3.1 ☐ ☐ PDR	5.1 ☐ ☐ PDR	7.1 ☐ ☐ (PDR)
	3.2 ☐ ☐	5.2 ☐ ☐	7.2 ☐ ☐ PDR
		5.3 ☐ ☐	7.3 ☐ ☐
			7.4 ☐ ☐
			7.5 ☐ ☐
			7.6 ☐ ☐

12b. Science activities: Living processes   1   2   3   4   5   6   7   NA

Y N	Y N	Y N	Y N
1.1 ☐ ☐ PDR	3.1 ☐ ☐ PDR	5.1 ☐ ☐ PDR	7.1 ☐ ☐ (PDR)
	3.2 ☐ ☐	5.2 ☐ ☐	7.2 ☐ ☐ PDR
	3.3 ☐ ☐	5.3 ☐ ☐	7.3 ☐ ☐
			7.4 ☐ ☐
			7.5 ☐ ☐
			7.6 ☐ ☐

12c. Science activities: Food preparation   1   2   3   4   5   6   7   NA

Y N	Y N	Y N	Y N
1.1 ☐ ☐ PDRQ	3.1 ☐ ☐ PDRQ	5.1 ☐ ☐ PDRQ	7.1 ☐ ☐ P
	3.2 ☐ ☐ PDQ	5.2 ☐ ☐ PDRQ	7.2 ☐ ☐
	3.3 ☐ ☐	5.3 ☐ ☐	7.3 ☐ ☐
		5.4 ☐ ☐	

DIVERSITY SUBSCALE

13. Individual learning needs   1   2   3   4   5   6   7

Y N	Y N	Y N	Y N
1.1 ☐ ☐ PQ	3.1 ☐ ☐ PQ	5.1 ☐ ☐ PQ	7.1 ☐ ☐ Q
1.2 ☐ ☐ P	3.2 ☐ ☐ P	5.2 ☐ ☐ P	7.2 ☐ ☐ P
1.3 ☐ ☐ P	3.3 ☐ ☐ R	5.3 ☐ ☐ R	7.3 ☐ ☐ P RQ
1.4 ☐ ☐ R	3.4 ☐ ☐	5.4 ☐ ☐ (D)	7.4 ☐ ☐ PDR

14. Gender equality and awareness   1   2   3   4   5   6   7

Y N	Y N	Y N	Y N
1.1 ☐ ☐ D	3.1 ☐ ☐ D	5.1 ☐ ☐ D	7.1 ☐ ☐ PQ
1.2 ☐ ☐	3.2 ☐ ☐	5.2 ☐ ☐ (Q)	7.2 ☐ ☐ Q
		5.3 ☐ ☐ (PQ)	7.3 ☐ ☐ Q

15. Race equality and awareness   1   2   3   4   5   6   7

Y N	Y N	Y N	Y N
1.1 ☐ ☐ D	3.1 ☐ ☐ PDR	5.1 ☐ ☐ (P)	7.1 ☐ ☐ PDRQ
1.2 ☐ ☐ D	3.2 ☐ ☐ D	5.2 ☐ ☐ D	7.2 ☐ ☐ PDRQ
		5.3 ☐ ☐ PD	7.3 ☐ ☐ Q
		5.4 ☐ ☐ Q	

53

Profile ECERS–E

Centre/School: _____   Observation 1: __ __ / __ __ / __ __   Observer(s): _____
                                                        d d   m m   y y

Teacher(s)/Classroom: _____   Observation 2: __ __ / __ __ / __ __   Observer(s): _____
                                                        d d   m m   y y

	1	2	3	4	5	6	7	

I. Literacy Subscale
(1-6)

Obs. 1 [ ]   Obs. 2 [ ]

Average sub-scale score

1. Print in the environment
2. Book and literacy areas
3. Adult reading with the children
4. Sounds in words
5. Emergent writing/mark making
6. Talking and listening

II. Mathematics Subscale
(7-9b)

[ ]   [ ]

7. Counting and the application of counting
8. Representing simple numbers
9a. Shape and space
9b. Sorting, matching and comparing

III. Science and environment Subscale
(10-12c)

[ ]   [ ]

10. Natural materials
11. Areas featuring science/science resources
12a. Science processes: Non Living
12b. Science processes: Living processes
12c. Science processes: Food preparation

IV. Diversity Subscale
(13-15)

[ ]   [ ]

13. Planning for individual learning needs
14. Gender equality and awareness
15. Race equality and awareness

Average Subscale scores

LITERACY
MATHEMATICS
SCIENCE AND ENVIRONMENT
DIVERSITY

1 2 3 4 5 6 7

Appendix A: Overview of the Subscales and Items of the ECERS-R

Space and Furnishings
1 Indoor space
2 Furniture and routine care, play and learning
3 Furnishing for relaxation and comfort
4 Room arrangement for play
5 Space for privacy
6 Child-related display
7 Space for gross motor play
8 Gross motor equipment

Personal care routines
9 Greeting/departing
10 Meals/snacks
11 Nap/rest
12 Toileting/diapering
13 Health practices
14 Safety practices

Language-Reasoning
15 Books and pictures
16 Encouraging children to communicate
17 Using language to develop reasoning skills
18 Informal use of language

Activities
19 Fine motor
20 Art
21 Music/movement
22 Blocks
23 Sand/water
24 Dramatic play
25 Nature/science
26 Math/number
27 Use of TV, video and/or computers
28 Promotimg acceptance of diversity

Interaction
29 Supervision of gross motor activities
30 General supervision of children (other than gross motor)
31 Discipling
32 Staff-child interactions
33 Interactions among children

Programme and Staff
34 Schedule
35 Free play
36 Group time
37 Provision for children with disabilites

Parents and staff
38 Provision for parents
39 Provision for personal needs of staff
40 Provision for professional needs of staff
41 Staff interaction and cooperation
42 Supervision and evaluation of staff
43 Opportunites for professional growth

Appendix B: Reliability and validity in the ECERS-E

The ECERS-E was developed specifically for assessing curricular aspects of quality, including pedagogy, in pre-school centres subject to the national Early Childhood Curriculum for England. Multi-level statistical analyses revealed that quality of centre-based provision as measured by the ECERS-E was a significant predictor of children's development at entry to school after controlling for pre-test, child characteristics and family background (Sylva *et al*, 2006). As demonstrated in the EPPE (http://eppe.ioe.ac.uk) and the Millennium Cohort (http://www.cls.ioe.ac.uk/studies.asp?section= 000100020001) studies (Mathers et al., 2007c), the ECERS-E is a reliable and valid instrument for assessing the educational aspects of process quality and is a significant predictor of children's cognitive, linguistic and social-behavioural development.

The ECERS-E curricular extension scales were developed for the EPPE research project specifically to address the educational/curricular aspects of 'quality', which are assessed in less detail in the ECERS-R (Sylva *et al*, 2006; Soucacou and Sylva, in press). It is generally accepted that when some new measure is developed, the measure should be tested for validity and reliability (Bryman and Cramer, 1990). Validity refers to the capacity of the new instrument to measure what it purports to measure – and not something else. In other words, a measure is valid if carrying out all its procedures leads to an accurate assessment of the idea or the concept it is trying to measure. Reliability refers to the consistency of a measure. There are two types of consistency: the first asks whether two or more observers would come up with the same score on the same day (consistency across observers) and the second concerns how the items relate to each other. The reliability and validity of the ECERS-E scale were established as follows:

Criterion validity

A measure is said to have criterion validity if scores on it are very similar to scores on another agreed instrument for measuring the same concept. Thus, criterion validity seeks agreement between a theoretical concept (what you are trying to measure) and a well-known measuring device or procedure that has been used successfully in the past (Bryman and Cramer, 1990). Criterion validity of the ECERS-E scale for the UK has been successfully demonstrated by a study of 141 pre-school settings (Sylva *et al*, 1999; Sylva *et al*, 2006). The correlation coefficient between total scores on the ECERS-R and the ECERS-E was 0.78, indicating a strong positive relationship between the two measures. Even though the two instruments focus on somewhat different dimensions of the pre-school settings, they both measure a general construct of 'quality'. Therefore, it is expected that centres obtaining a high score on the ECERS-R will obtain a moderate-to-high score on the ECERS-E. However, there are still differences in what the two scales measure and that is why the correlation is not 1.00, which would indicate that they measure exactly the same thing.

Apart from the high correlation between the ECERS-E and the ECERS-R, criterion validity of this new scale has also been established through the strong relationship with the Caregiver Interaction Scale (CIS), a scale for assessing the quality of relationships between setting staff and children. Sammons and her colleagues (2002) report significant moderate correlations between the ECERS-E total and two CIS subscales: 'positive relationship' ($r = .59$) and 'detachment' ($r = .-45$). The correlation coefficients between all the ECERS-E subscales and the CIS subscales ranged from low to moderate, with the positive relationship subscale being moderately associated with all ECERS-E subscales (from .45 to .58).

Predictive validity of the construct (children's outcomes)

Predictive construct validity refers to the extent to which the scale predicts scores on some measure that can be theoretically deduced to relate to the new measure. For example, higher quality centres should have children in them who make more developmental progress over time than centres with lower scores. In the case of the ECERS-E, quality scores of the centres predicted the developmental progress (gains between pre-test at age 3 and post-test at age 5) of children in the EPPE sample. The predictive power of the ECERS-E in relation to cognitive progress was found to be better than the power of the ECERS-R in predicting progress of 3,000 children. Controlling for a large number of child, parent, family, home and pre-school characteristics, the ECERS-E total was significantly associated in a positive direction with pre-reading scores, early number concepts and non-verbal reasoning. The literacy subscale had a significant positive effect both on pre-reading and on early number concepts. In addition, non-verbal reasoning was predicted by the maths subscale of the ECERS-E and the diversity subscale. The diversity subscale also had a significant positive effect on early number concepts. As for the behavioural outcomes, there was a trend (just missing significance at .05) for the ECERS-E to predict independence/concentration and co-operation/conformity (Sammons *et al*, 2003).

In an attempt to compare the size of the contribution of the ECERS-E and ECERS-R scores in predicting children's cognitive and social/behavioural outcomes, effect sizes were calculated following the method developed by Tymms, Merrell, and Henderson (1997). Effect sizes are important as they enable comparison of different predictors. These are presented in Table 1.

Table 1: Effect sizes of ECERS-R and ECERS-E total and subscale scores on cognitive and social/behavioural outcomes (after controlling for child, family and home environment characteristics) (Sylva et. al., 2006).

	Cognitive outcomes					Socio-behavioural outcomes			
	Pre-reading	General Mathematical Concepts	Language	Non-Verbal Reasoning	Spatial Awareness	Independence & Concentration	Co-operation & Conformity	Peer Sociability	Anti-social/ Worried
ECERS-E									
Total	0.166[a],*	0.163*	0.076	0.108*	0.023	0.120#	0.124#	0.073	-0.038
Literacy	0.174*	0.142*	0.059	0.105	-0.028	0.097	0.124#	0.077	-0.040
Maths	0.127	0.102	0.042	0.142*	-0.041	0.054	0.077	0.090	0.028
Science/ Environment	0.012	0.105	0.091	0.109#	-0.056	0.111#	0.079	0.034	-0.059
Diversity	0.138#	0.165*	0.033	0.191*	-0.018	0.113#	0.117#	0.021	-0.046
ECERS-R									
Total	0.085	0.087	0.083	0.042	-0.044	0.089	0.131*	0.009	-0.094
Space and furnishings	0.068	0.008	0.065	0.022	-0.019	0.009	0.103	-0.033	-0.108
Personal care	-0.024	0.028	0.083	-0.057	0.042	0.055	0.128	0.026	-0.086
Language and reasoning	0.104	0.090	0.067	0.053	-0.108#	0.096	0.148*	0.030	-0.065
Activities	0.015	0.062	0.074	0.062	-0.065	0.046	0.067	-0.029	-0.028
Interaction	0.080	0.199*	0.053	0.073	-0.037	0.134*	0.180*	0.116#	-0.059
Programme Structure	0.063	0.035	0.041	0.037	-0.064	0.033	0.064	-0.018	-0.049
Parents and staff	0.144#	0.014	0.045	0.045	0.008	0.054	0.087	-0.012	-0.071

[a] When change of centre is not included in the model   * p<.05   # p<.08

The significant and moderately strong relationship between the ECERS-E and children's cognitive development suggests that important elements of the educational/curricular environment measured in the ECERS-E scale are related to children's development. This, in turn, validates this instrument as a measure of quality related to 'emerging' academic skills as well as social/behavioural development (Sylva *et al*, 2006).

The ECERS-R appears to be a more sensitive measure of quality related to children's social-behavioural development, while the ECERS-E assesses quality relating to children's cognition and their 'academic' skills. The fact that the two scales predict cognitive and social progress over the pre-school period in different ways suggests that different aspects of children's development are being measured. Consequently, if academic achievement is valued at the start of school, the ECERS-E is a good predictor of children's readiness for school (in relation to language, numeracy, and literacy skills). In a cultural context where the development of social skills is considered most important, the ECERS-R is a better measure of a good start at school, at least in England.

Concurrent validity of the construct (Qualifications of staff)

Further criterion validity of the scale was established by examining the association between observed quality and the qualifications of staff. Theoretical considerations would predict that staff with higher qualifications would be found in centres of higher quality. Construct validity of the ECERS-E scale was established in the Millennium Cohort Study (Mathers, Sylva and Joshi, 2007). A random sample of children in the MCS who attended group care was selected at the age of 3 and permission sought to visit the centres they attended and carry out the ECERS-R, ECERS-E, and CIS observations. Information was collected on a number of centre characteristics with the aim of establishing which centre characteristics were related to, and predicted, quality of provision. The ECERS-E was used to measure the quality of provision in literacy, maths, science, diversity and equality plus the overall quality of curricular provision. The childcare qualifications of staff working in the rooms observed were an important predictor of ECERS-E scores in 301 centres in the MCS (Mathers *et al*, 2007a). Analyses revealed that, after controlling for a variety of centre characteristics (including size, ratio and type of centre), the mean qualification level of all staff had a significant effect on quality scores; it was significantly related to the total and to all subscales of the ECERS-E. The *beta* weights shown in Table 2 represent the degree to which staff qualifications in each of the 300+ centres predicted the ECERS-E scores.

Table 2: Relationship between mean staff qualifications and ECERS-E scores

ECERS-E subscale	Standardised β	p value
Total ECERS-E score	0.21	< .001
Literacy	0.25	< .001
Maths	0.15	< .05
Science	0.18	< .01
Diversity	0.13	< .05

The findings from the Millennium Cohort study suggest the ECERS-E has concurrent validity. Qualifications were most strongly related to the 'literacy' subscale of the ECERS-E suggesting that higher qualifications are related more to literacy than to other aspects of the curriculum (Mathers et. al, 2007a).

Inter-rater reliability

In the EPPE study (Sylva et al, 1999), inter-rater reliability on the ECERS-E was calculated from data obtained from the 25 randomly chosen centres that were also used in the factor analysis of the ECERS-R. The reliability coefficients were calculated separately for different regions of the country, both percentages of exact agreement between the raters and as a weighted kappa coefficient. The percentages of inter-rater agreement range from 88.4 to 97.6 and the kappas range from 0.83 to 0.97, indicating very close agreement between raters. Similar high levels of agreement were found in the Mathers et al study (2007a).

Factor analysis and internal consistency

Factor analysis conducted on the ECERS-E in 141 centres (Sylva et al, 2006) indicated the presence of two factors that together account for about 50 per cent of the total variance in the scores. The first factor has been named Curriculum areas and the second Diversity. Table 3 presents the items that load (higher than .6) on these two factors.

Table 3: Two factors in the ECERS-E (N = 141 centres)

Factor 1: Curriculum	Loading	Factor 2: Diversity	Loading
Environmental Print letters and words	0.684	Gender equality	0.763
Natural materials	0.683	Race equality	0.702
Counting	0.678	Book and literacy areas	0.643
Science resourcing	0.656		
Talking and listening	0.649		
Sounds in words	0.634		

A Cronbach's alpha was calculated for each factor; this was high (0.84) for Factor 1, and moderate (0.64) for Factor 2. The alpha values show that the two factors have moderate to good internal consistency.

Scores on the validating sample on ECERS-R and ECERS-E

The mean total score from the 141 centres on the ECERS-R was 4.34 (SD =1.00) and 3.07 (SD =1.00) on the ECERS-E. The former score is in the 'adequate to good' range whilst the latter indicates 'adequate' quality. Table 4 shows the total and subscale score on both scales.

Table 4: Total and subscale scores on ECERS-R and ECERS-E from the validation sample (n=141 pre-school centres; Sylva et. al., 2006)

	Mean	SD
ECERS-R		
1. Space and furnishings	4.85	1.04
2. Personal care routines	3.81	1.36
3. Language and reasoning	4.32	1.33
4. Activities	3.83	1.16
5. Interaction	4.82	1.31
6. Programme structure	4.70	1.47
7. Parents and Staff	4.07	1.28
Total ECERS-R	4.34	1.00
ECERS-E		
1. Literacy	3.96	1.06
2. Mathematics	2.95	1.19
3. Science and environment	2.98	1.52
4. Diversity	2.38	1.11
Total ECERS-E	3.07	1.01

Quality across nations and cultures

The concept of 'quality' is not universal; it is influenced by national curricula and cultural priorities. The outcomes thought to be important in children's development will relate in different ways to different measures of quality. If academic achievement is valued at the start of school, then the ECERS-E is a good predictor of children's readiness for school. This readiness includes language, numeracy skills, the component skills of early literacy, and scientific understanding. However, the social interaction scale on the ECERS-R may be a better predictor of a child's strong start at school if social outcomes are valued. The social outcomes related most to the ECERS-R were children's independence and cooperation/conformity.

The ECERS-E was developed in England, although its structure was greatly influenced by the ECERS-R, which was developed in the US. It has proved valid in other European countries (e.g., Rossbach, in preparation), and its authors welcome discussion with those who use it for research or professional development around the world.

References

Arnett, J. (1989) Caregivers in Day-Care Centres: Does training matter? *Journal of Applied Development Psychology*, 10, 541-552.

Bryman, A., and Cramer, D. (1996). *Quantitative data analysis with minitab: A guide for social scientists* Routledge.

Harms, T., Clifford, R.M. and Cryer, D. (1998) *Early Childhood Environmental Rating Scale, Revised Edition (ECERS-R)* Teachers College Press.

Harms, T., Clifford, R.M. and Cryer, D. (2003) *Infant/Toddler Environmental Rating Scale-Revised (ITERS-R)* Teachers College Press.

Harms, T., Jacobs., E.V., White. D.R. (1996) *School-Age Care Environmental Rating Scale (SACERS)* Teachers College Press.

Harms, T., Cryer, D., and Clifford, R. M. (2007) *Family child care environment rating scale revised edition (FCCERS-R).* Teachers College Press, 88.

Mathers, S. and Sylva, K. (2007a) *National Evaluation of the Neighbourhood Nurseries Initiative: The Relationship between Quality and Children's Behavioural Development, Sure Start Research Report SSU/2007/FR/022.* London: DfES/ Department of Educational Studies University of Oxford.

Mathers, S., Linskey, F., Seddon, J. and Sylva, K. (2007b) Using quality rating scales for professional development: experiences from the UK. *International Journal of Early Years Education*, 15:3, 261-274 URL: http://dx.doi.org/10.1080/09669760701516959

Mathers, S., Sylva, K. and Joshi, H. (2007c) *Quality of Childcare Settings in the Millennium Cohort Study.* DSCF Research report SSU/2008/FR-025. London: DCSF.

Office of National Statistics: http://www.statistics.gov.uk/default.asp

Office for Standards in Education (Ofsted) (2008) *Early years self-evaluation form guidance: Guidance to support using the self-evaluation form to evaluate the quality of registered early years provision and ensure continuous improvement.* Reference No 080103 London available at www.ofsted.gov.uk

Qualification and Curriculum Authority (QCA) (2000) *The Foundation Stage Curriculum Guidance. Qualifications and Curriculum Guidance Association.* London.

Rossbach, H.G. (in preparation). *Using the ECERS-R in German pre-school centres.*

Sammons, P., Sylva, K., Melhuish, E., Siraj-Blatchford, I., Taggart, B. and Elliot, K. (2002) *Measuring the impact of pre-school on children's cognitive progress over the pre-school period. Technical Paper 8a.* London: Institute of Education.

Sammons, P., Sylva, K., Melhuish, E., Siraj-Blatchford, I., Taggart, B. and Elliot, K. (2003) *Measuring the impact of pre-school on children's social behavioural development over the pre-school period. Technical Paper 8b.* London: Institute of Education.

Siraj-Blatchford, I. (2002a) Final annual evaluation report of the Gamesley Early Excellence Centre. Unpublished report, University of London, Institute of Education

Siraj-Blatchford, I. (2002b) Final annual evaluation report of the Thomas Coram Early Excellence Centre. Unpublished report, University of London, Institute of Education

Siraj-Blatchford, I., Sylva, K., Muttock, S., Gilden, R. and Bell, D. (2002) *Researching Effective Pedagogy in the Early Years (REPEY) Study*, London: DfES Research Report, 356.

Isley, B. J. (2000) *The Tamil Nadu Early Childhood Environmental Rating Scale (TECERS)*, M.S. Swaminathan Research Foundation, Chennai, India.

Sylva, K., Melhuish, E., Sammons, P., Siraj-Blatchford, I., and Taggart, B. (2008) *Final report from the primary phase: pre-school, school and family influences on children's development during Key Stage 2 (age 7-11)*. DCSF RR 061. Nottingham: Department for Children, Schools and Families.

Sylva, K., Melhuish, E., Sammons, P., Siraj-Blatchford, I., and Taggart, B. (2004) *The Effective Provision of Pre-school Education (EPPE) project: Final report*. A longitudinal study funded by the DfES 1997-2003.DFES Nottingham

Sylva, K., Siraj-Blatchford, I., Melhuish, E., Sammons, P., Taggart, B., Evans, E., Dobson, A., Jeavons, M., Lewis, K., Morahan, M. and Sadler, S. (1999). *Characteristics of the centres in the EPPE sample: Observational profiles. Technical Paper 6*. London: Institute of Education.

Sylva, K., Siraj-Blatchford, I, Taggart, B., Sammons, P., Melhuish, E., Elliot, K, and Totsika V. (2006) Capturing quality in early childhood through environmental rating scale. *Early Childhood Research Quarterly* 21 76-92 Elsevier

Tietze, W., Cryer, D., Bairrao, J., Palacios, J., and Wetzel, G. (1996) Comparisons of observed process quality of early child care and education in five countries. *Early Childhood Research Quarterly*, 11(4), 447-475.

Tymms, P., Merrell, C., and Henderson, B. (1997) The first year at school: A quantitative investigation of the attainment and progress of pupils. *Educational Research and Evaluation*, 3(2), 101-118.

Yan Yan, L. and Yuejuan, P. (2008) Development and validation of Kindergarten Environment Rating Scale. *International Journal of Early Years Education*, 16(2), 101-114.